Road Grace

Road Grace

Essays for a New Renaissance

John Newmeyer, Ph.D.

BRIGHT MOON PRESS
San Francisco

First edition published by Bright Moon Press,
2004 Gough Street, San Francisco, California 94109

Library of Congress Catalog Number 20-02095109

Newmeyer, John. Road Grace.

ISBN 0-9641233-1-2

CONTENTS

I. Social and Physical Health

Road Grace 3
Lighting a Candle 4
Antivisible Man 6
Public and Private Theft 9
Tent People and Blanket People 11
Advice First, Then Money 15
Beggar's Brass Bowl 18
The Ethanol Gardens 21
Consuming Passions 25
A Brief History of the After Sobriety Movement 30
Junkies' Rental Rights 36
On Contradiction 37
Good Cop, Bad Doc 43
Three Outrageous Notions 45

II. History

The Servants' Century Off 53
Stern-Men and Bow-Men 55
The Institute for Policy Negation 57
Evaporation 60
Mobutu Letter 66
A Correspondence on Prohibition 68
Blood on Their Hands 71
What We Have Gained 73
What We Have Lost 76

III. Class

How to Tell if You're "Old Money" 85

Toward an Hereditary Upper Class 87
Climbing Beacon Hill 92
Ten Commandments for a Ruling Class 97
Poor Day, Rich Life 99
AIDS and Class 106
Sick and Poor, Sick and Rich 110

IV. The Gay World

Alphabet of Gaydom 119
Telephone Strategies as an Impediment to Homoerotic Love 124
Finishing Golden Boys 127
Cock Size in Gay Escorts Ads 130
Short and Tall Men Together 134
Prevention for Gay Men 139
A Modest Proposal 142
Stories from the Closet 147

V. Fun and Games

The Innocent Pleasures of Adulthood 153
Ten Symptoms of Employee Burnout 155
Eulogical Workplace 156
Zeno at the Intersection 158
Five-Handed Bridge 161
Seven-Handed Bridge 164
Periodic Table of the Greatest Culinary Elements 165
Intergalactic Purr 166
How to Distinguish a Cat Lover from a Cat Fanatic 167
Syllabus 169
Why Can't a Dog Be More Like a Cat? 171
Pets and Spiritual Health 177

ACKNOWLEDGMENTS

In each year since my first book (*August 32, 2000 and Other Essays for a New Millennium)* came out in 1994, I've written 20 to 25 essays. Early in 2002 I had the notion that there were enough good ones for a second book. I assembled all these new essays in a great pile, and promptly put aside 90 of them as "too esoteric", "too weird", or just plain "naaah..."

That left 60 essays that I *thought* might be worth sharing with the world. But the judgment of wise friends was needed. So, thanks to the gimlet eyes of Newton Butler, John Finn, Rory Hopkins, Greg Johnson, Peel Leifer, Peter Pursley, and Michael Rossoff, ten more essays were tossed out, leaving just 50 for this collection.

Thanks to the patient and skillful support of Cathy Purdy and Alan Worley of BookMasters, I've been able to metamorphose a mere manuscript into this hardcover tome. I commissioned a talented Estonian artist, Sergei Minin, to create the painting upon which the cover art was based.

Great thanks are also due to John Teton, whose constructive prodding has kept me at my writing and at many another worthwhile enterprise in my life. Also, great thanks to David Crowther for advancing my comfort and competence with computer software and hardware, and to Linda Brown for doing the final editing.

DEDICATION

To the reader who chances across this book at the end of the Third Millennium, I have three hopes: first, that *homo sapiens* has learned to live lightly upon the Earth, in numbers fewer than ten billion, and with tender regard for the plants and animals with whom we share this magnificent planet. Second, that your civilizations have come to love learning for its own sake, so that people never lose a childlike curiosity. And third, that kindness and justice prevail in all human interaction.

This book is dedicated to all Earth-travelers who, at the outset of the Third Millennium, are helping to fulfill one or another of these three great hopes. They are the artisans of a new Renaissance.

FOREWORD

In a world of disorder and aggression,
here is carefulness and dignity.

In a time of rudeness and confusion,
here is an interval of good sense and clarity.

In a society without moorings,
here is a vision of sanity and security.

In a culture insufficiently appreciate of life–
of the wonders of human connection–
of the pleasures of bed, table, and mind–
here is John Newmeyer,

Or at least a part of him in words on paper
in a book that will make you think.

--Randolph Delehanty

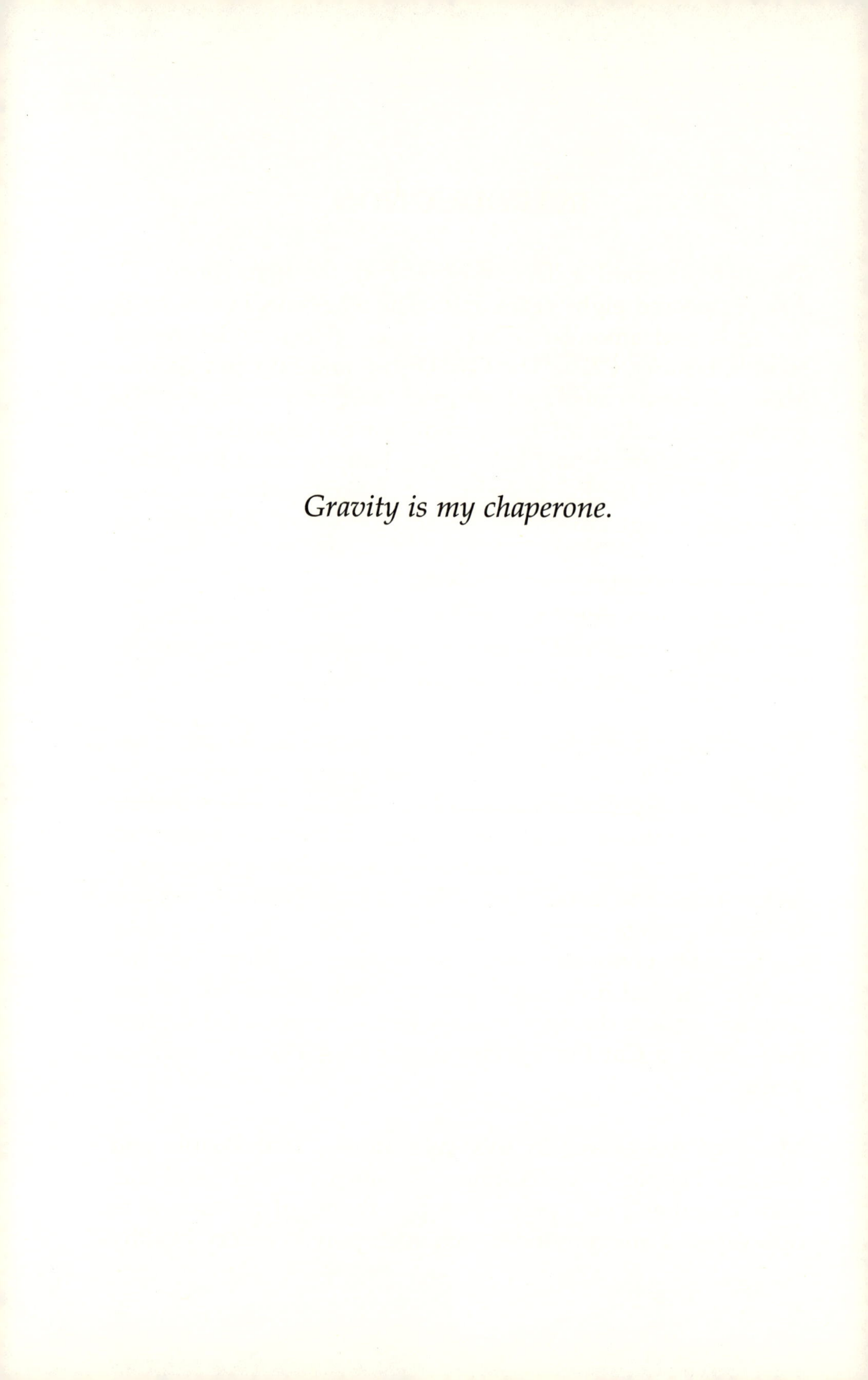

Gravity is my chaperone.

INTRODUCTION

This is my second collection of essays; the first, *August 32, 2000*, appeared eight years ago. The 50 essays in this book are sectioned among five topic areas: Social and Physical Health, History, Class, The Gay World, and Fun and Games. Most of these consist of whimsy and wry humor. The remainder are little attempts on my part to make the world a more livable place– including some long pieces at the end of Sections I and III that were part of my professional work as an epidemiologist in the grand struggle against HIV disease.

Except for "Cock Size in Gay Escorts Ads", none of these works has been published before. However, most of them– and many others– can be found in cyberspace at the website (www.newmeyer.com) I launched in 1997.

The images on the front covers of my two books are polar opposites. On *August 32, 2000*, we saw a cat, indoors, at night, in an Apollonian scene of introspection and scientific inquiry. On this book, we see a dog, outdoors, on a glorious summer day, expressing a Dionysian flow of extraversion, forgiveness, and good cheer. The change between the two reflects a change in my own life: more outgoing, more optimistic, more connected with humanity, more (dare I say it?) *doglike*. As Carl Jung might put it, in the second half of our lives we explore the opposite of what had dominated the first half– thus, a Cat Person becomes a Dog Person, and vice versa.

Many of the essays in this collection– "Tent People and Blanket People", "Consuming Passions", "Short and Tall Men Together", etc., play upon this theme of the comity of opposites. I am convinced that such play is a very healthy thing– perhaps even an urgent necessity– in these times. I love the notion that the Mediterranean climate here in California– cool, wet, green, and feline from November to April, and warm, dry, golden, and canine from May to October– annually plays out the dance of opposites. It's a metaphor for the real work we all need to do: to achieve a little closeness, a little comity, with the Other, the Alien, the Unexpected. My hope, dear reader, is that these essays just might perk you up for this great dance.

John Newmeyer, Ph.D.
San Francisco
October 2002

I.

SOCIAL AND PHYSICAL HEALTH

"Lighting a Candle" is my call to launch a 'virtuous circle' against litter in the streets. "Antivisible Man" explains that people we don't want to see are more than merely invisible; they occupy a strange kind of 'negative space'. "Public and Private Theft" argues that it's far easier to 'steal' from the faceless public than from a private individual. In "Tent People and Blanket People", the rich and the poor each have criteria for a successful evening by the Opera House. "Advice First, Then Money", "Beggar's Brass Bowl", and "Ethanol Gardens" are my commonsense solutions to homelessness, begging, and public inebriation. "Consuming Passions" puts America's eight favorite psychoactive drugs (four legal, four not) on the table for a closer look. "Brief History" speculates upon a world where sobriety is a valuable commodity, exchangeable on the free market for 'life therapy' vouchers. In "Junkies' Rental Rights" we find people (o horrors!) using pay toilets to shoot up, and maybe they have a right to do so... Next are four pesky "Contradictions" which beguile our war against HIV. "Good Cop, Bad Doc" argues that cops will get better, and doctors worse, at providing social services like HIV prevention. Finally we have "Three Outrageous Notions"– about the Great Pox and chastity, the persistence of fast-lane sexual behavior, and the impotence of drug abuse treatment.

Hear now a word about Dreamtime, that enchanted time of year when certain laws of human society are suspended.

During Dreamtime, the conflicts of family life are replaced by love and nurturance; music achieves sweet transcendence and brings tears to the eyes; rich foods do not fatten, nor does strong drink intoxicate; the coldest, darkest, wettest days merely increase the joys of home and hearth. Nearly everyone in these Northern climes falls under the spell of Dreamtime– it comes upon one slowly and seductively, fully suffusing one's being by the middle of December.

One awakens from Dreamtime around the sixth of January, as if from a profoundly restorative sleep, refreshed and energized for the new year...

Road Grace

I find that the pleasures of driving in California– the fine weather, the beautiful scenery, the exquisite Classical music on my car's CD system– often put me in a very cheerful mood. In such a frame of mind I muse, "How good the world has been to me— I'm keen to pass on these blessings to other people!"

I have discovered that I don't need to wait until I arrive at my destination to act upon these philanthropic impulses. I can *actually do so as I drive.* There are drivers wanting to pull into my lane; there are other drivers hoping to make a left turn; there are pedestrians wanting to cross safely; and if I'm very lucky, there'll be someone with a disabled car who needs help. Yes, there are as many as 50 occasions in an hour's driving where my desire to show kindness and courtesy can be satisfied.

Of course I'm not the only one like this– there are millions of drivers on the road in California every day, looking for opportunities to do as I'm doing. We need a name for this mass phenomenon. I suggest that we call it "Road Grace".

Lighting a Candle: How One Citizen Copes with Litter

People complain because the streets of their city are littered. I answer, "better to light a candle than curse the darkness." I light that candle by going after litter in a couple of small areas.

There are three elements to my work. First, I concentrate on just two blocks in my hometown of San Francisco: the one where I live and the one where I work. I pick up litter on each block once a week– usually Tuesdays by my home and Fridays by my workplace.

Second, I use a couple of simple tools: a large brown paper bag and a "grabber" that I bought at a hardware store for $9. With this "grabber"– in effect a pair of tongs at the end of a long stick– I can quickly nab a piece of trash without having to stoop or get my hands dirty.

Third, and most important, I let myself be satisfied with 90% success. I work quickly, not minding if I miss a few pieces. This way it takes me only 6 minutes to pick up 90% of the litter that's on the block. Had I spent twice the time, I'd get 98%– but the marginal gain is not worth the effort. And that's why I think brooms and dustpans and thoroughness are the wrong approach: it takes too long to do each block to perfection, and the worker is discouraged because the litter soon returns.

My work is light, so it's been easy for me to keep at it, week after week. Within the first month I found myself in a virtuous circle: just as litter encourages littering, the lack of litter inhibits people from littering. So each week I find a little less trash on my block, which means I can use my 6 minutes' commitment to clean part of the next block.

People stop to thank me and– sometimes!– to inquire where they can obtain a "grabber".

My leverage is enormous. In each of my two blocks, I constitute perhaps 2% of the habitants, but my weekly commitment to cleanness has made all the difference. Only a tiny proportion of San Francisco's citizens need to follow my example before our virtuous circles coalesce as a "tipping point", and the whole city suddenly finds itself notably more free of litter.

Antivisible Man

In his extraordinary book, *The Invisible Man,* Ralph Ellison elaborated upon the "invisibility" of blacks in America. His notion is that most whites do not want to see black people for what they are, and therefore "look right through them as though they were invisible," whether in physical encounters on the street or in the metaphorical ways in which the society's peoples are visualized.

I believe that something even more extreme, the *Antivisibility phenomenon,* comes into play in certain circumstances. Here, so powerful is the desire of the viewer not to see the object that his eyes are literally constrained from directing his view toward the object. The purpose of this constraint is not merely "not to see" but also *not to make eye contact.* Here are three examples of the Antivisibility phenomenon:

Beggars. Everyone who lives in an American city of any size encounters them regularly. Seeing them is a noxious experience, but being obliged to acknowledge them is several times more noxious. Hence, the tactic of forceful not-seeing, thus to deter the interrogative, "Spare change, please?" The pedestrian employs the Antivisibility strategy, allowing his eyes to look *anywhere* but where the beggar is.

Cruisers. This is a scene most familiar to young singles searching for erotic partners. A typical American "on the cruise" makes three successive sensory judgments on each person encountered:

(1) "Is the person of a suitable race, sex, and age-range for me?"; if "Yes", then,

(2) "Is he/she attractive?"; if "Yes" again, then,

(3) "Is he/she interested in me?"

My research shows that only 6% to 20% of those persons getting a "Yes" on (1) also get a "Yes" on (2). Even then, to get a "Yes" on (3) requires that oneself gets a "Yes" on (1) and (2) from the other person, a condition which may have a low probability. Fortunately, the three judgments can all be made in a fraction of a second, largely through eye gymnastics– and in a well-attended cruising environment, hundreds of people can be so judged in an hour.

The Antivisibility phenomenon comes into play when Person B is obviously attracted to Person A, who is in turn not attracted to Person B. It is then in A's interest to avoid any eye contact with B, because such contact may encourage B to begin a conversation and thus waste A's precious cruising time. The consequence is that many people at a cruising scene render themselves Antivisible simply by their hungry eye movements, which– in a fraction of a second and almost without conscious awareness– cue the objects of their interest to "look not there, or there, or there!" Cruisers who are homely can in this way become subject to massive Antivisibility. Contrariwise, very attractive persons can find the space so rife with "look not there!" forbidden spots that their eyes have almost nowhere to rest; this may result in a form of blindness or a panicky desire to flee...

Glitterati. People of high social status periodically gather at upper-class tribal rituals, such as opening night at the Opera, the Royal Enclosure at Henley, or the Cotillion. As in any other social scene, participants hobnob with their good friends and ignore strangers. But what about those of nearly-equal social status with whom one is merely acquainted?

This is a keen issue when there is a lot of milling-about and one encounters the same acquaintances again and again. Many people, but especially upper-class people who have much social business to transact and deplore wasting time, adopt a three-stage strategy: a polite "hello, how are you?" on first encounter, a cursory nod on the second encounter, and– on the third and subsequent encounters– the exercise of Antivisibility, of "eyes, look not there!"

I propose a method of testing the Antivisibility phenomenon. If my hypothesis is true, the existence of a Target of Antivisibility– a beggar, for example– should create a blind spot of a certain size, perhaps a circle 5° or 10° in radius. That means that an object within the radius of Antivisibility but not obscured by the Target would not be seen by the observer. The test would consist of placing something that would normally be readily noticed– a nude woman, for example– in the distance behind, and at a 2° radial distance to the left of, the head of an imploring beggar. If Antivisibility is real, the nude would not be noticed, whereas mere invisibility would allow her to be seen. By this method we may be able to prove the existence of a phenomenon even more radical than that described by Ralph Ellison.

Public and Private Theft

A friend of mind— let us call him Brian— taught me a powerful lesson about communism the other day. He had expressed to me his admiration of a certain Marky Mark poster, and boasted of his exploit in "appropriating" one of them from a bus kiosk here in San Francisco. I asked Brian if he would have "appropriated" the poster from someone's living room if he could have gotten away with it; he answered "of course not!" and indeed seemed startled by my question. I explained that it struck me that the sum-total loss of esthetic pleasure by the citizenry was probably much greater in the case of the public as opposed to the private poster; but Brian simply replied, "Oh, they'll replace the poster that I took!"

This interaction— I shall always think of it as "my epiphany from Brian"— demonstrated the important distinction between the "they" (as in "they'll replace the poster...") whose public property can be abused with impunity, and the "he" whose private property is sacrosanct.

Another example can readily be seen by observing the brown United Parcel Service vans as they conduct the day's business on the streets of a city. It takes the UPS driver an average of three minutes to deliver a package; what is worth noticing is *where* the van is parked for that interval. Often the driver has two alternatives, equally convenient for him: to pull into a nearby driveway, or to double-park in a nearby traffic lane. Now, in three minutes' time, it is unlikely that the driveway's owner will be inconvenienced, but it is quite likely that several drivers will find their traffic lane blocked and will be obliged to change lanes. Yet the UPS driver will almost always make the latter choice, because it feels so much safer to offend the anonymous public citizenry than a specific private citizen. The strategy chosen by UPS (and by truck and van drivers in general) damages the overall public welfare many times more than the alternative would, and yet it will prevail, because the alternative contains the great deterrent of the keen and heartfelt, albeit rare, outrage of the private citizen.

A third example can be found in the phenomenon of graffiti. Note the prevalence of graffiti in your city: how much of it is on public property, and how much on private? My own informal survey disclosed that most was on public property, such as buses, bus stops, park walls, and freeways. Most of the remainder was on "corporate" property, such as the sides of large buildings. Interestingly, public housing accounted for the bulk of defacement of residential property. I believe that the tag artist operates under the same ethics as the UPS driver: never mind the faceless public, but beware the outrage of the private property owner.

Communism was the great failed utopia of the Twentieth Century; even the Germans couldn't make it work. The examples I've cited give a glimpse into the key reason for that failure: governments simply can't get people to respect public property as much as private property.

Tent People and Blanket People

Each September the "Tent People" of San Francisco gather for two gala banquets— the first on Wednesday after Labor Day, to celebrate Opening Night at the Symphony; and the second two days later, for the Opera's Opening Night. At each event the gentry are feted under large tents, set up for the purpose in the parking lots off Franklin Street.

The Host Committee for the Tent People have a daunting task. They must make sure that the tent environment provides all of these amenities:

- Adequate shelter
- Attractive lighting
- Commodious chairs and tables
- Handsome interior decor, such as a sumptuous display of flowers
- *Carefully* thought-through seating arrangements for the guests
- Tasty food, served at the right temperature
- Appropriate beverages before, during, and after dinner
- Prompt and efficient service and bussing
- An entertaining but not overlong program, as well as

background music

- A sound system suited to that program
- Bathroom facilities for the gentlemen and (especially) the ladies
- A security force to let the right people in and keep the wrong ones out

If the Committee fails its duty in regard to even *one* of these amenities, many of the Tent People will consider the evening badly marred, even ruined. If as many as three of the amenities are badly muffed, the consensus will be that the evening was a disaster, to be mentioned in outraged tones for years afterward, with members of the Committee shunned or mocked. (The reader who doubts this should randomly select three from the above list, and conduct a thought experiment...)

While the hundreds of Tent People are being attended to, an even larger company of homeless people are coping with the later parts of their September day in the City— some of them less than a minute's walk from the Tent. These folks often wrap blankets around themselves as a simple deterrent against the evening cool; hence my description of them as "Blanket People".

The Blanket People also have a list of things that they might look forward to on a September day:

- A safe, warm, dry place to shelter
- A long, hot, sudsy bath

- A really good meal
- Effective treatment for their disease symptoms
- A shampoo and haircut
- A shave
- A manicure and pedicure
- A comfortable night's sleep in a soft bed
- A set of clean clothes
- The companionship of an old friend
- A twenty-dollar bill
- An apartment with the month's rent already paid

Now, if even one of these amenities comes to pass, it will "make my day!" for the lucky homeless person. If— Lord bless!— three of these were to happen, it would be a day of such good fortune as to be remembered fondly for years.

But consider this marvelous feature of human nature: there are some Tent People for whom three or more amenities could be muffed, and their enjoyment of the evening, though altered, would overall not be a bit less. And there are some Blanket People whose sense of wretchedness would not be lessened if three, or six, or even all, of the amenities from their list came their way.

Gender is a major factor. It is the women who drive the agenda at Tent People events; the men seem rather out of place, as if they were being swept along by an irresistible tide. Contrariwise, the world of the Blanket People is a man's world, with the female minority playing their part with apparent passivity and reluctance. Perhaps because of their minority roles, the Tent men are far more likely than the women to suffer missing amenities with cheerful insouciance— while many of the Blanket women have a crone-like inability to appreciate however many amenities may come their way.

Tent People or Blanket People, male or female, the human condition is a shared one: around eleven PM most of these People will manage a long, satisfying gulp of wine and a reflection along these lines, "Well, another long day in this amazing City of ours— Lord, how sore my feet are!"

Advice First, Then Money

In the heyday of the Welfare State the phrase was often heard, "the poor need money, not advice!" We were urged not to impose our values upon poor people, but rather to help them redress their poverty with a maximum of cash benefits. Even the idea of giving food vouchers to panhandlers was under suspicion as "judgmental".

It's time to question all of that. The keynote for a new attitude should be, "It's important to get money to the poor, but let's be sure they get their money's worth!" Or, "advice first, then money." Most of this advice could have come from anyone who coped with the Great Depression:

- **Be willing to move.** As the saying goes, "the poor come and go, but the rich go on and on." That's because the rich are stuck where they are, tied down by their investments in local real estate and businesses. The poor have no such anchors. This means they're free to Get Out of Dodge when times are bad, and emigrate to where jobs are plentiful and rent is cheap– such as Riverside where there are lots of jobs for the unskilled and one-bedroom apartments are $400 a month. Let the rich stay, and stagnate!

- **Live communally.** What a premium we pay to live alone, in our studios and one-bedroom apartments! Even sharing with two others cuts costs by nearly half, for example $225 per person in a three-bedroom apartment in Riverside. Of course, one has to pick the right roommates and get along; the advantage goes to those with a thick skin and a good sense of humor...

- **Buy in bulk.** Once in a multiple-person household,

the obvious next move is to shop at Costco rather than the neighborhood market. The savings on food and other household goods are close to 50% (see p. 100). Lack of transportation or storage space can be an impediment, but cars can be borrowed ("we'll fill the tank") and space can be found under tables and beds.

• **Form, or join, cooperatives.** The obvious cooperatives are for food and housing, but there are creative ways to travel, to co-own cars, and to share childcare responsibilities. But if one can stomach religion, a community of faith is just the thing– especially one of Jews, or Episcopalians, or Mormons, where the poor are scarcer. Aside from the alms, there's a cozy sense of community.

• **Love libraries and reading.** Leave the Opera, the Symphony, the nightclubs, and Las Vegas for those with money to blow. The public libraries are still free, and hold rich stores indeed for the active imagination. Or, if passive entertainment is preferred, a thousand classic movies are there to be rented and shown on the home VCR– with friends asked to join in, "and by the way, bring some refreshments."

• **Despise clothes.** An image: bundles of secondhand clothes sold in Nairobi for a few dollars per *hundredweight*. America is awash in excess clothing. Goodwill stores are choked with the stuff. One can dress comfortably, even stylishly, for pennies on the dollar.

• **Volunteer at clinics.** Healthcare is the one part of the personal budget that's much costlier now, in real dollars, than during the Great Depression. If employee health benefits, or Medicare, aren't available, the best option is to volunteer at a community clinic. That will usually facilitate access to basic medical care, and also access to smart thinking about preventive medicine.

• **Just beer, please.** Let this be the only intoxicant, and only in the evenings. Substance use is a great drain on the wealth (and health) of the poor. Some can manage to abstain, but for most the best hope is to displace liquor, cocaine, cigarettes, etc., with good old beer. Stout or dark beer is actually not bad nutrition, and "lite" beer will help deter a weight problem. And it's the stuff of conviviality, and can be had for less than $1 a can at Costco.

• **Get involved in politics.** The greatest untapped resource in American politics is all those low-income citizens who don't bother to vote. What a difference they can make in close elections, such as November 2000! The goal is easily stated: "there shall be fewer Republicans in public office."

These points are so obvious that, far from being a set of ways to "act smart", they are a checklist of ways to avoid "being dumb". One can imagine Tom Joad rising from the dead to voice them– and there's no way *he* would be accused of condescension...

The Beggar's Brass Bowl

San Francisco has had to cope with beggars for decades. One coping approach is to hope that a combination of affordable housing, job training, mental-health care, and substance abuse treatment will help such people get their lives together. Another strategy is to refuse to give any money or help, in the hope that beggars will simply give up and go away. But nothing has changed; beggars seem as abundant as ever. It's time to consider a third approach, one which respects begging as a form of entrepreneurship which can be sensibly regulated to the benefit of all. The problem is to clarify the services provided by beggars, and to reduce the noxious aspects of their entrepreneurship.

I propose that we **license beggars** and issue them numbered **medallions**, much as we do for taxi drivers. Each medallion will display the owner's name and a small image of his face, and will be welded to a handsome **brass begging bowl**, the size of a half-cantaloupe. Coins dropped in these brass bowls will make a distinctive clang, an aural marker of charity: "the bells of almsgiving" to honor the almsgiver.

The bowl's medallion will certify the owner as legally registered. The registration system will enable the City to allocate beggars equitably among neighborhoods. Residents of a neighborhood can know by the medallion numbers which holders were assigned to their area (for example, #311 to #320 for Glen Park.) Thus, almsgivers can discriminate in favor of "their" neighborhood's beggars, and against those not in their assigned areas.

Medallion-holders will gain by caring for their neighborhood in little ways. They can pick up trash, remove graffiti, help drivers avoid parking tickets, tend to street trees, and so forth. They can be "street concierges", helping the neighborhood keep its public areas clean and safe. To the extent they did these jobs well, they will find local almsgivers more generous.

The brass bowl and medallion will be a thing of great value to a beggar: the beginnings of private ownership. Without it, he won't get much, as the public will discriminate frankly against unlicensed "gypsy" beggars, just as they do against "gypsy" cabdrivers. A beggar will vigorously protect his bowl, even to the extent of chaining it to his waist.

The great gains for the beggar are the dignity and privileges conferred by possession of his bowl and medallion, with his name and face proudly displayed. Among these privileges could be a personal storage locker, vouchers for brief use of a place to clean up, an assigned mailbox at the local post office, and automatic voter registration at the local precinct. These privileges could help him stay cleaner and less obtrusive, which would further increase almsgivers' generosity.

The great gain for the rest of us is that the begging population can be allocated fairly among the whole of San Francisco. Soon enough, the idea will commend itself to the rest of the country, and the entire mendicant citizenry of America can be equitably allocated.

Two vexing questions arise: who will be given preference for medallions? and how will fraud be prevented? It's probably best to give preference to mendicants who have lived most of their lives in the area, and/or to those who truly can't get an income either through work or welfare. As for fraud prevention, there's probably no better measure than a clear photograph indelibly attached to the medallion and bowl.

By redefining begging as a "street concierge service", with rewards for providers who are competent and minimally noxious, we can go far toward re-integrating thousands of individuals into society. Of course, we must recognize that some people aren't able to cope with life outside of institutions.

The Ethanol Gardens: A Proposal for Alcohol Maintenance

I ask you, dear reader, to envision an "Ethanol Garden" near the downtown of your city. The Ethanol Garden was created for public inebriates: people who are inclined to get drunk every evening, but who lack the means or inclination to do so in private. The Garden is enclosed by high walls, within which is a large area partly under the open sky and partly sheltered. There are ample chairs, tables, toilets, storage lockers, and sleeping facilities.

Clients seeking admission to the Garden enter through the white north door. Only individuals previously registered as public inebriates may be admitted, and only by means of an electronic "handprint identifier" unique to each client. Clients may enter any time between 6 PM and midnight, but once inside must stay until the next morning.

The alcohol is dispensed as nearly-pure, 190-proof ethanol. It is available from 7 PM to shortly after midnight at a "bar" in the center of the Garden. Clients must pay cash for their ethanol, but it is provided by the Federal Government *tax-free* and *overhead-free.* That is, the only expense to the user is the actual cost of production of the ethanol: about $1.20 per gallon or 1 cent per ounce. Clients purchase their ethanol in ounce units, up to five ounces for a nickel; they rarely need more than 15 cents to cover their nightly "costs". Most clients prefer to dilute, and a variety of mixers– tasty, nutrient-rich fruit juices– are provided free for that purpose.

After the clients consume their desired quantity of alcohol, they make use of comfortable cots and blankets to sleep off their inebriation. This nightly client community polices itself quite nicely most of the time, even more so than traditional hobo communities. The Ethanol Garden has the advantage that shortages of alcohol, the major source of conflict among hoboes, never occur.

Clients may leave anytime between 8 AM and noon. A simple but hearty breakfast is available for those so desiring. Each departing client must make an important choice among three exits: the green south door, the golden east door, or the black west door. Each exit has a specific meaning and design, derived from Native American culture:

South Door (Green)	*"I will carry on as always"* A simple exit to the outside world.
West Door (Black)	*"I am sick, I need help"* A passageway, furnished with items of the undertaker's and gravedigger's crafts (coffins, winding cloths, headstones, etc.) leading to a clinic where minor ailments can be treated and major ones referred out.
East Door (Golden)	*"I've had enough of this life, I want to get sober"* A desk where the client is given a seven-day dose of Antabuse and enrolled in a 12-Step program, to the accompaniment of applause and cheering. Also, a counter where sets of clean clothes are available for free.

Once a city has an Ethanol Garden, the whole debilitating process of the inebriate's life– wandering about, begging, purchasing booze, consuming in public, passing out in public, being taken to the 'drunk tank'– is brought under one roof and transmuted into a far pleasanter experience for all. There is immediate relief from most of the nuisances of public inebriation. Just one such nuisance, "begging for booze money", is so noxious that its amelioration will promptly commend the Garden to the public.

Of course, there's a clandestine, "hiding away" aspect in creating a walled garden– but interested citizens can learn about its goings-on through vivid newspaper and television reportage. Citizens and clients alike will appreciate the frankness and directness of the pricing scheme which shows that alcohol is, in fact, ridiculously *cheap*. Also, the rich symbolism of each morning's exit– choosing among the three doors– gives an epic quality to the inebriate's life and reminds him that he has some control over his path in the grand scheme of life. Each morning, he chooses either to continue as before, to acknowledge that alcohol is slowly poisoning his body and hastening his death, or to seize the hope for a Recovered life.

* * * * * * * *

There are no Ethanol Gardens quite yet. But what a noble experiment to create just one, if only to expose three great fallacies:

Fallacy One: "Booze is expensive". No way! Booze is dirt cheap; it's the flavoring, packaging, wholesaling, retailing, advertising, taxes, and other puffery and exploitation that turns a pennyworth of ethanol into a three-dollar vodka cocktail.

Fallacy Two: "Boozers can't help it". Maybe in past decades they were helpless, but not any longer– not in the age of Antabuse and Alcoholics Anonymous. Millions of "boozers" of all sorts choose every day to be sober.

Fallacy Three: "A community of boozers can't govern itself." Maybe not in the long run, but good governance only needs last the night's bout. If the few real needs– safety, shelter, warmth, food– are abundantly supplied, governance will take care of itself, and supplies can be replenished in the afternoon. (It would be wise, nonetheless, to have a separate Gardens for men and women. And at the door, weapons should be checked and musical instruments lent out freely.)

A single successful Ethanol Garden might be enough to explode a fourth fallacy: that we must resign ourselves, year after year, decade after decade, generation after generation, to all the nasty aspects of public inebriation.

Consuming Passions

After long years of studying substance use and abuse, I've realized that only eight "substances" really matter. There are of course marijuana, heroin, cocaine, and "speed", the four major illicit *drugs*. Looming over these are alcohol, tobacco, caffeine, and sugar, the four great legal drugs (a.k.a. *foods, beverages, substances*.)

The few who use illicit drugs seem to pursue the same psychoactive effects as the many who make do with the legal drugs, roughly thus:

Psychoactive Effect Sought	Illegal Drugs	Legal Drugs
Stimulation, a "pick me up"	Cocaine, "Speed"	Caffeine, Tobacco
Comfort, relief from pain, "attitude adjustment"	Heroin	Alcohol
Sheer pleasure, a gladdening of spirit	Marijuana	Sugar

Recently I conducted a fascinating exercise: I put a month's "supply" of each substance on a table to see what they'd look like together. I found data in the almanac on the nation's consumption of the legal substances, and I also located recent D.E.A. estimates on consumption of the four illegal drugs. Then I calculated the average American monthly consumption of the 8 substances, by dividing overall consumption by population. For sugar and caffeine, I divided by the total population of 281 million, and for the other substances I divided by the total adult population of 214 million. Here are the results, expressed in milligrams per month per American:

SUGAR (pure)	5,900,000 mg.
ALCOHOL (100 proof)	750,000 mg.
CAFFEINE (coffee beans)	380,000 mg.
TOBACCO (cigarettes)	210,000 mg.
MARIJUANA (leaves)	300 mg.
COCAINE (pure)	125 mg.
SPEED (pure)	15 mg.
HEROIN (pure)	5 mg.

This "standard American monthly consumption", once assembled on the table, looked like this: the sugar was in 13 one-pound cartons, the alcohol was in a fifth of 100-proof vodka, the coffee was five-sixths of a pound of beans, and the tobacco was 149 ordinary cigarettes. The illicit drug consisted of marijuana leaves equal to about one-third of a cigaretteful, the cocaine was 1/32nd of a teaspoon of powder, the speed was about 1/8th of the cocaine amount, and the heroin about 1/3rd of *that* amount.

The table groaned under the weight of the sugar. The vodka, cigarettes, and coffee were also weighty, a pound or so each. But the marijuana leaves, about the volume of a cashew-nut, were almost lost in this pile of consumables. And the cocaine, speed, and heroin were of derisory insignificance, little scatterings of grains rather like what you'd see on the table if you knocked over a salt shaker.

This exercise was a vivid reaffirmation that America's drug scene is totally dominated by the four legal drugs. We notice the four illegal drugs mostly because the relatively tiny minorities who use them are vigorously and conspicuously persecuted.

How Much Do We Pay?

When I purchased the four legal drugs, I was surprised to notice that *I paid the same amount* for each "monthly per capita share": about $7, excluding taxes. Of course there were no taxes on the sugar and coffee, but Federal and State taxes just about doubled the price of the vodka and more than tripled the price of the cigarettes. Thus, after hundreds of years of competition among growers, refiners, wholesalers, and retailers, the before-tax price of a month's worth of each of the four main drugs has come down to about an hour's wage for an unskilled worker. I reflected on that as I gazed at my tableful of legal drugs: how marvelous that so many pick-me-ups, so much warmth and comfort, such ample gladness of spirit, is to be had so cheaply in our times!

This thought soon gave way to melancholy reflection upon the four illegal drugs. The street costs of the amounts shown in the table are also not far from $7 per person per month, but that's a population-wide average: in reality, maybe 1% or 2% of adults are regular users and each spends about fifty or a hundred times as much. Presumably they get the same basic psychoactive effects as the rest of us do from the legal equivalents, but more intensely so (after all, they're smoking crack rather than drinking coca tea, while we're sipping coffee rather than snorting caffeine powder.) They do so in the face of great tribulations, and usually manage to keep at it only so long as the stamina of youth endures. Then they rejoin the rest of us in a docile middle age of Starbucks and doughnuts, booze and Marlboros.

In the Aggregate

The above table can also serve as a handy measure of overall American consumption, simply by replacing "milligrams" by "tons" and changing "monthly" to "every four months" (for sugar and coffee) or "every five months" (for the other six substances). For example, the aggregate American consumption of sugar is 5,900,000 tons every four months; of cocaine, 125 tons every five months. It immediately becomes obvious that commerce in the legal drugs is characterized by huge amounts of sheer labor: millions of people to pick the winegrapes and coffeebeans, staff the factories, drive the trucks, shlep the cases of booze around, restock the supermarket shelves, etc., etc. The amount of labor needed for the marijuana, cocaine, speed, and heroin industries is trivial by comparison. Yet *every one of these eight drugs is a multibillion dollar industry* in America in 2002. It is obvious, therefore, that the profit margins on the illegal drugs are far greater, if only because the billions in income are distributed among far fewer workers. But there were also big profit margins for coffee, tea, sugar, and tobacco in the 17th and 18th centuries: planters and shippers became fabulously rich because they served insatiable demands of consumers who craved the new pleasures and eagerly paid good money for them.

What Are the Consequences for HIV and HCV?

Gazing again at my tableful of drugs, I see three legal ones that are eaten or drunk, plus a fourth legal one which is smoked. A prodigious amount of illness and premature death is blamed upon these four substances, starting with 400,000 deaths per year from tobacco and 100,000 from alcohol in this country alone. The mortality from the illegal drugs is by comparison tiny, but in the past decade the greatest part of it resulted from AIDS, and in the new century the greatest part will probably come from hepatitis-C. Here are the annual averages for the 1990s:

Deaths from HIV infections which resulted from injection drug use	15,000
Accidental deaths (overdoses, etc.) resulting from use of illegal drugs	5,000
Drug-related murders	1,000
Drug-related suicides	<1,000

To which we can add annual averages starting around 2010:

Deaths ultimately resulting from HCV transmitted via injection drug use	5,000

I have long argued that the problem of illegal drugs can be resolved by "legalize, tax, regulate, and discourage". I would like to see illegal cocaine and heroin replaced by legal coca tea and laudanum (see "A Short History of the Conquest of the Crack Epidemic" in *August 32, 2000*.) With milder forms of the drug, swallowed rather than injected, there would be no HIV or HCV infection and far fewer overdose deaths. Moreover, there would be no legions of inner-city youth imprisoned, alienated, and disenfranchised. But– sweet irony!– the "tableful of substances" could groan all the more with the pounds of coca-leaf tea and laudanum bottles, all costing just a few dollars of the future citizen's earnings, but adding their own share to morbidity and mortality consequent upon long-term regular use...

A Brief History of the After Sobriety Movement

April 2007

San Francisco's After Sobriety movement was inspired by Yvonne Williams, a young crack abuser who in 1996 finally resolved to quit the drug. With the help of a support group of like-minded women, she managed to stay clean, but was frustrated in getting enough help to put her life back together. The critical moment came at a public hearing in the Spring of 1997, when Ms. Williams angrily declared, "we've done our job, we've cleaned up, why can't you help us?...we just can't relate to your treatment programs– give us better choices!" Hearing this, the City's officials were inspired to realize, "My God, *these people possess a commodity which the public is willing to buy*. Why not enable them to exchange it on the free market and give them the power of choice?"

That commodity is *sobriety*, a manifest benefit to substance users' families, neighbors, and community, as well as to themselves. The great innovation of the City back in 1997 was to "pay" for this commodity in vouchers– vouchers to use as a medium of exchange by people in recovery.

The After Sobriety movement helped San Francisco to create a new strategy against substance abuse, composed of three parts: self-help "Groups" of people committed to being clean and sober; "Visiting Staff" providing all kinds of services needed "after sobriety"; and the City, regulating and coordinating the whole system.

The Groups

Sobriety groups are the foundation of the system, the bedrock support for abstinence and recovery. There are now more than a thousand such groups. There are Native American Groups, teenage Groups, senior citizen Groups, ex-con Groups, computer-nerd Groups, Salvadoran refugee Groups, Laotian Groups, even a "leathermen stockbrokers" Group. Many formed by slow accretion of friends and acquaintances, many found their members through the Internet, some were organized by psychotherapists, some simply arose from the culture of the streets. Many Groups operate on Twelve Step principles, others are frankly Christian or Muslim, still others are simply rap groups. Some meet every day, some only once a week; the average is three or four meetings per week. Some are as small as nuclear families, others have nearly 100 members; the average size is 12. But all the Groups share one thing: a conviction that substance abuse is destructive, and that abstinence is the only real hope. A few of the groups permit themselves a little beer or wine, but most commit to avoiding *all* intoxicating substances, legal or illicit.

The "culture of honesty" is absolutely central to the Groups' identity. Honesty is *the* paramount cultural virtue; as Yvonne Williams puts it, "Better a truthful old white guy than a lying sister!" Group participants are razor-sharp– and ruthless– at detecting lies or "slips". And because the Groups offer things of great value quite apart from the Vouchers– friendship, intimacy, and community– their participants are motivated to adhere to the norm of sobriety, much more so than they would be in any treatment program.

With the help of Project Open Hand, the Groups are able to

nurture their participants in a quite basic way: delicious hot meals at most of the meetings. Generous support from the City enabled Open Hand to adapt to the decline of HIV-related needs, and start serving a different population. These meals have proved to be *very* valuable morale boosters.

In the Groups, people learned to like and trust one another. This has enabled a great many of them to team up and rent large apartments and flats, sharing costs. By thus forming "extended families of choice" to obtain housing, one pressing problem of "how do we get our lives together, after sobriety?" has been largely solved. But what about the many other needs of people beginning lives in recovery? These needs are addressed by Vouchers.

The After Sobriety Visiting Staff

Beginning in 1998, the City issued "After Sobriety Vouchers" to all participants of registered Groups. These Vouchers could be freely exchanged for a wide variety of needed services:

- Vocational counseling
- Psychological counseling
- Stress reduction counseling
- Urban life skills counseling
- Medical care
- Childcare
- Adult education

More than a thousand "After Sobriety Visiting Staff" are now registered to provide these services. The "Visiting Staff" are just that: they come to the clients, rather than waiting for the clients to come to them. Their middle-class traits of owning cars, keeping appointments, being on time, etc., suit them well for their work: most of it consists of arriving at an appointed time (usually the end of a scheduled Group meeting) to provide services to the Group members, either collectively or individually. For these services the Visiting Staff are given Vouchers, which they can in turn exchange for something of value: salaries and fringe benefits. The more Vouchers earned, the higher the salary.

The Vouchers quickly solved the problem of cultural competency: if you weren't able to relate to the folks in a Group, you weren't invited back. Those that were competent at least with some Groups, thrived. Visiting Staff annual earnings range up to $80,000, and up to $120,000 for physicians. Surprisingly, the most successful have been middle-aged Latinas, who are particularly in demand by groups of young men struggling to overcome "speed" abuse. In the early days of After Sobriety, these women were so in demand that they made *big* money, but eventually the supply increased to meet the demand.

The morale of the Visiting Staff is generally high. Especially attractive is the variety and challenge of the tasks, and the flexibility to work as many or as few hours as desired. Even the physicians enjoy a role reminiscent of the traditional family doctor, carrying his black bag and making house calls...

The City's Role

The City's main jobs, through its Internet Substance Abuse Systems (ISAS) office, are to keep a registry of Groups, to run the Vouchers system, and to certify the basic skills of the Visiting Staff. The City also provides space, free of charge, in its buildings for the Groups' meetings. Finally, the City regularly monitors the system to expand the parts that are working and redesign the parts that are not.

Moneys to pay for the Vouchers system originally came from the City's substance abuse treatment funding. As treatment program staff quit to register for the more lucrative and enjoyable Visiting Staff jobs, and as clients deserted for the more relevant Sobriety Groups, the City's treatment programs gradually atrophied and shut down, thus freeing funding. But the huge success of the new system required more funds. Beginning in 1999, these were raised by City taxes on alcohol and tobacco, amounting to about a dollar per quart of whisky, and a quarter per pack of cigarettes. After marijuana was legalized in 2003, it too was taxed. Polls show that the San Francisco citizenry is pleased that "substance users are paying the downstream costs of their abuse." There is currently a lot of pressure to regulate cocaine, heroin, and other drugs so that they, too, can provide tax revenue; but so far the only real revenue these drugs provide to the Vouchers program is through seizure of drug traffickers' assets. Even so, the system will operate at a net gain to the City in Fiscal Year 2007: $77 million will be raised in alcohol, tobacco, and marijuana taxes, but the Voucher system and its administration will only cost $68 million.

An Overview

In retrospect, we failed to predict back in 1997 how quickly San Francisco's substance abuse strategy would be renewed by the system described above. We expected a lot of resistance from entrenched interests, but it just evaporated. The line staff of the treatment programs jumped at the opportunity to escape the stifling confines and endless paperwork of "The Program" and go freelance. The program executives were at first resistant, but soon realized that they too could redefine their work: now they specialize in harm reduction outreach to the (smaller but still sizable) population of abusers not in recovery. As for the San Francisco Police Department, it grudgingly agreed with Brendan Behan that

> There is no manifestation
> of addictive disease
> That cannot be made worse
> by the involvement
> of a police officer

and was thankful for a new climate in which substance use was mostly decriminalized.

Had we, ten years ago, reflected on the worldwide failure of centrally planned *economies*, we might have realized, as we do now, that centrally planned *social service systems* are also inclined to fail. We began to sense something was wrong during the 1997 public hearings on "Treatment on Demand", which became so mired in a tangled swamp of internal contradictions, reams of information, and "huge needs everywhere." It took the cry for empowerment of a young Black woman to focus us on the greatest need of people in recovery: consumer choice in a free market.

Junkies' Rental Rights

May 8, 1999

Editor
San Francisco *Chronicle*
Fifth and Mission Streets
San Francisco, CA 94103

Dear Editor:

Your article "Junkies Shooting Up in S.F. Public Toilets" (May 3) implied that we should be horrified at such deviant use of "public" property. However, the user of the toilet is in effect a tenant, paying cash for the use of a certain space (80 sq. ft.) for a certain time (20 minutes)– a high rental rate, equivalent to $90 for a day's use of a 400 sq. ft. motel room, or $5,400 for a month's use of an 800 sq. ft. apartment. If a tenant causes no disturbances during his tenancy and vacates the premises in good order, should we mind what happens in his temporary private space? Or is private rental space purchasable only for middle class naughtiness, such as adultery in motels and potsmoking in apartments?

Sincerely,

John Newmeyer

On Contradiction

Contradictions play a big role in the wars on substance abuse and HIV, especially as regards people with "dual diagnoses". Here are four of the most prominent contradictions:

Overwhelming Needs v. Limited Resources

AIDS experts, on occasion, have attempted to compile a complete "Wish List". When the experts address the full range of needs of people living with HIV (symptomatic or not) plus people at risk for HIV infection, that List can be very long indeed. Given the politicization of AIDS, the List is apt to be replete with "shoulds" and "musts" and an undertone of anger at a society which appears unresponsive and uncaring. One need not know the name of this Commission or that Task Force, but merely visualize the scene of the deliberations: the roomful of professional and community leaders, the earnest discussions, the big sheets of paper on the wall, the care to make every voice heard...

Substance abuse experts make Lists too, albeit more rarely. Recently, I participated in a "Planning Council for Substance Abuse Treatment on Demand" sponsored by the San Francisco Department of Public Health. A lot of our work consisted of naming all the resources and services that might ideally be provided so that a maximum number of substance abusers could get maximum benefit from relevant treatment. We ended by listing nearly 100 interventions, some genuinely new but most just applying existing modalities to as-yet-unserved populations.

There's a fundamental contradiction: our Lists are long, but the required money, political will, and other resources are short.

The two best ways to resolve this contradiction, in my experience, are ranking and expanding the pie: "Yes, we know the List is long. All of the needs we've specified should be addressed. But here is our ranking in order of which ones should be tackled first." And also, "Listen, Mr. President [Congressman/Governor/Supervisor], these measures are pretty much all cost-effective– the taxpayer will get much more back in a richer, healthier, more flourishing society than is paid in taxes. So please add an extra million dollars so that we can work our way further down that prioritized List!"

Treatment on Demand v. Culturally Appropriate Treatment

The cheapest way to achieve "substance abuse treatment on demand" is to open programs for each of the proven modalities (outpatient detox, outpatient drug-free, methadone maintenance, therapeutic community, etc.), train staff to run them, let the substance abusers know of the treatment sites, and wait for them to show up for admission. In this scheme, dollars can be allocated at so much per "slot"– $5,000/year for a methadone "slot", $2,000/year for an outpatient detox "slot", etc.– and excess "slot capacity" can be budgeted so that there's rarely a wait for admission.

The major problem with this strategy is the assumption that, for slots, "one size fits all." At any one time, a big proportion of drug abusers– perhaps a majority– are unwilling to enter treatment, and for many of them, the reason is some variant of, "I can't relate to that program!" San Francisco has done much to resolve this problem, for example by establishing programs for women or for monolingual Spanish speakers– i.e., "culturally appropriate" treatment.

A contradiction arises when we attempt to enhance "treatment on demand" and "culturally appropriate treatment" simultaneously. In promoting the latter, there is the possibility that dozens of programs within each treatment modality would need to be set up, each serving a cultural subpopulation. But to be able to provide treatment on demand, all of the programs would have to have excess slot capacity. That would be hugely more expensive than furnishing the treatment modality as a whole with excess slot capacity.

How much more expensive? A crude model gives an idea: suppose a city has an average of 1,000 admissions in a modality per treatment cycle, and wants to provide enough excess capacity to handle an overload of up to 40%. Suppose further that this excess capacity is adequate for 9 out of 10 cycles. A "one program fits all" strategy will require 400 extra slots; but if there are ten programs for ten distinct subpopulations, a total of roughly 630 extra slots will need to be funded. Then there are the additional fixed costs of operating ten different programs rather than one; variable costs are presumably about equal.

It would help if we could agree whether culture is generally learned or inherited. That is, do we adopt the "French version", which holds that a person of any ethnicity is French once certain essential patterns of language, belief, attitude, and behavior have been mastered? Or do we hold to the "German version" which insists that a person, however adept at German culture, cannot be German without a minimum of "German blood"? If we adopt the "French version", it might resolve the contradiction described above: program staff could be trained in cultural sensitivities far beyond the culture(s) they were born into. In effect, "one size fits all" could be made to work because the staff are made to adjust to the clientele rather than vice versa.

Another way to resolve the contradiction is to organize services around the free market rather than through central planning (see "A Brief History of the After Sobriety Movement", p. 30.) If people in need are empowered with vouchers, the fundamental locus would be the "sobriety group" rather than the "clinic", and demand would create supply.

Middle-Class Staff v. Lower-Class Clients

In general, Americans are fascinated by race but in denial about class. The result has been a peculiar blindness about a very important contradiction in substance abuse treatment: the great majority of staff are middle-class and the great majority of clients are lower-class. But much of the work between staff and clients is about class: making and maintaining treatment plans, retooling for gainful employment, achieving residential and family stability, and so forth. If there is such a thing as class conflict, surely it exists in the treatment program setting.

This contradiction is less prevalent in the HIV treatment field because so many clients are middle-class. But in class terms, the HIV clientele– even in San Francisco– is gradually becoming more like the substance-abuse clientele (see "AIDS and Class", p. 106.)

One way to resolve this contradiction is cultural sensitivity training sessions for staff with social class as the focus.

Participants would examine their own values about education, job stability, homeownership, the nuclear family, planning and saving for a future, etc., and think through their relationships with people that don't now– and might never– share those values. Participants could come to accept that there is integrity in class identities other than the bourgeois. A treatment staff enlightened in this way could provide more effective and relevant help to the clientele.

The Culture of Sobriety v. the Culture of Intoxication

Even when middle-class staff work with middle-class clients, or lower-class staff with lower-class clients, an important contradiction may be at work. Treatment staff are generally part of a "culture of sobriety" engaging in uncompromising war against the "culture of intoxication" and demanding that clients abandon the latter culture in favor of the former.

This contradiction is probably inevitable and resolved only by local victories of the "culture of sobriety". Ethnographic studies of substance users, however, show that those victories may be slow in coming: many users find "the life" sustainable, rewarding, and rich with human interaction and support. Early experiences of the Haight-Ashbury Free Clinics show that the contradiction can at least be transmuted from an antagonistic to a non-antagonistic one. The tactic of the HAFC in the late 1960s was to apply the notion of addiction more widely, as in, "America is hooked on sugar," "lots of us are addicted to cigarettes," or "I do counseling with speedfreaks but I myself am a coffee junkie!" The result was to reduce social distance between counselor and client: to see lots of "us" in "them", and of "them" in "us". The transmutation was from an antagonistic "doctor in white coat condescending to humble patient" to a non-antagonistic "peer counselor helping someone like me." We now see this as harm reduction: doing what we can to reduce negative consequences to individuals and communities, short of a complete victory for sobriety.

The contradiction also applies to safer sex as HIV prevention. It might be stated as, "The culture of chastity v. the culture of promiscuity." This conflict arises again and again in the world's fight against HIV disease, and unfolds much as with sobriety v. intoxication: the uncompromising war of the puritan against the libertine; local but not general victories for the puritans; the bewilderment that people should persist in promiscuous behavior in the face of viral "punishment"; the (rarer) achievement of a transmutation into a non-antagonistic contradiction.

Good Cop, Bad Doc

For as long as I can remember, junkies, speed-freaks and other druggies have liked doctors more than cops. Doctors– at least some of them– would lend a sympathetic ear to stories of pain and suffering, could understand that addiction was a disease and not a crime, and would not judge or punish. Cops, by contrast, were the epitome of "The Man": powerful, punitive, and implacably hostile.

Things may be very different in the 21st Century.

Physicians, in this new age of Managed Care, are increasingly part of a profit-oriented market system. To keep the bottom line of their provider network healthy, it's best if they provide as much as possible of highly specialized services. More and more, the ideal clinical setting is one where all the "prep work"– intake interview, blood pressure, getting the person oriented, etc.– is done by support staff. As many as a dozen patients can be prepped in a dozen different little rooms, and once prepped, the physician goes in to do his [expensive] specialized care, spending as little as 3 minutes, and rarely more than 15 minutes, with each patient. Assembly-line medical care such as this is highly efficient and cost-effective, and may be the best approach for a person who has a singular problem needing attention; but the typical addict has a complex of medical, emotional, and social problems that the 21st-Century doctor will simply be too rushed to deal with.

As such, doctors are seen by druggies as "not my kind"; they're part of the rich and privileged "overclass". They're absorbed in their high-technology profession, and simply not in touch with the street scene.

Policemen have their own new age, and it is all to the benefit of better relations with addicts: community policing, multicultural sensitivity training, and– increasingly– *de facto* decriminalization of drug use. More and more, cops will be trained to "know the neighborhood", to cope with all sorts of subcultures, to decide on the spot what petty crimes to overlook– indeed, to comprehend the whole urban context within which people carry on their lives. Moreover, from the druggies' point of view, a cop's role (Authority) may not be simpatico, but his social class (Blue Collar) is.

I hypothesize that the increasing advantage of cops, relative to docs, in dealing with the "whole person" will mean that cops will do more and better HIV prevention education than docs in the future. I believe my hypothesis will prove correct mainly because effective HIV prevention is ever more a sociological issue, and ever less a medical issue. That is to say, the street-level intervention that gets women away from abusive relationships, that tolerates needle exchange, that directs troubled people to the nearest detox clinic, that selectively busts nasty sex-club scenes rather than decent ones, will prove more effective than the clinic-room intervention that addresses viral load, immune-system functioning and venereal diseases.

We mustn't overlook all those support staff and paraprofessionals at the clinic who "prep" the patient to see the doctor. For the most part, they'll still have the time and the savvy to do effective HIV education, at places like the Haight-Ashbury Free Clinics.

Three Outrageous Notions

Below are three highly speculative ruminations on the subjects of HIV disease and substance use. Dear reader, I apologize if these notions seem too outrageous, but hey– it's a new century, and one's imagination is fevered...

(1) Smallpox, the Great Pox, and the End of the Single Standard

Background. From 1492, the peoples of the Western and Eastern Hemispheres were in regular contact with each other. A major result was the exchange of diseases. For the indigenous peoples of the New World, smallpox was the great annihilator: often nine in ten in a community would die, rendering the remainder helpless against the European colonists.

The peoples of the Old World, in turn, got hit by the Great Pox: syphilis. This disease first appeared among mercenary soldiers in Italy in 1494, possibly having been brought by Columbus' sailors. Syphilis raged with deadly ferocity through Europe during the Sixteenth Century. I believe that during this time the common people of Europe, mostly because of the terrifying impact of the Great Pox, shifted from a sexual Single Standard (sex before marriage is OK for both boys and girls) to a Double Standard (OK for boys but forbidden for girls.) Historians have hitherto overlooked this great shift, because they focus on written materials which mostly deal with the doings of the gentry and nobility and other literate classes. Of course richer Europeans always had a Double Standard: when a daughter has property worth inheriting, it's important to know who the father of her children are.

Hypothesis. I propose that a similar thing is happening right now: HIV disease is the syphilis of the new millennium, the deadliest sexually-transmitted disease (STD) to come along in 500 years. As such, it will cause many of the remaining Single Standard societies of the world to shift to the Double Standard. In particular, I predict that young women in Brazil, southern Africa, and Thailand– three notably "sex positive" regions– will shortly find that premarital chastity is the norm. Their virginity will be a matter for "protection", much as in the conservative (especially Catholic) societies of Europe from the Sixteenth Century onwards.

Safer sex for the educated classes is a matter of pamphlets and hygiene lectures and admonitions of wise elders. With the uneducated masses, learning is more at the gut level: when an STD begins to kill them in big numbers, an aversion to sexual liberties arises within a generation or so. Boys can never be kept from playing around, but with girls, a great ice age of chastity can set in and remain for a long time. Such an ice age is imminent for Brazil, southern Africa, Thailand, and many other regions now in the last days of an Indian Summer of the Single Standard.

Testing the Hypothesis. Watch for big drops in pregnancies and STD's (including HIV) among unmarried young women in the abovementioned regions, beginning about 2005.

(2) Young Fools, Old Fools, and HIV Disease

Background. In 1997 I started noticing paradoxical findings from San Francisco and Europe: people under 30 were becoming proportionally rarer among new AIDS diagnoses in the 1990s. It was as if young people had more successfully shifted to "safer" practices than had older people. Recent data from Alameda County reaffirm the paradox:

Age Range	AIDS Cases, 1981-1996	AIDS Cases, 1997-1998
13 to 29	706 (14.7%)	41 (12.2%)
30 to 39	2,043 (42.6%)	139 (41.5%)
40 and up	2,057 (42.8%)	155 (46.3%)

As can be seen, newer AIDS cases are on average older than earlier cases. Given that the rule, "young people careless, older people cautious" applies for every other disease transmitted by sex or by needle, what's going on?

An insight came to me at Thanksgiving, during a conversation about music with my young cousin. She expressed her love for heavy metal and I for Mozart; she joked, "Oh, it's 'cause you're older that you like that classical stuff!" I answered that age has nothing to do with it: I loved Mozart when I was twenty, and she would no doubt love rock when she's fifty. Then it struck me: maybe the same is true for HIV risk-taking, for the minority that are in the fast lane. The Fast Lane minority keeps engaging in risky practices well into middle age; the Non-Fast Lane majority have a moderate rate of risky practices in youth, which steadily declines as they age. As Gabriel Rotello suggests in *Sexual Ecology*, the way to overcome HIV in the gay community is to influence young gay men such that an ever-smaller proportion choose the Fast Lane.

Hypothesis. Fast Lane gay men continue to practice unsafe sex throughout their 20s, 30s, and 40s; they have sex mostly with other Fast Lane men of their own age; and as time goes by their sex partners are steadily more likely to be HIV+. As a result, HIV seroconversion rates do not decline with age, at least until 50. The same hypothesis can be made for intravenous drug users and unsafe needle practices, in regard to hepatitis-C as well as HIV.

Here's a model of the future of HIV disease to illustrate the hypothesis:

	Fast Lane 25%		Non-Fast Lane 75%	
Age Range	Annual Incidence	HIV+ at end of Range	Annual Incidence	HIV+ at end of Range
17-27	1.5%	15%	.2%	2.2%
28-38	2.0%	32%	.1%	3.3%
39-49	2.5%	49%	.05%	3.8%

Note that, though the "fast lane" people may be having less unsafe sex as they get older, the fact that they're still doing so, and amidst a population whose HIV+ rate increases, enables their seroconversion rate actually to increase. A formula to predict annual seroconversion runs thus:

$$\text{Annual seroconversion} = N_a \times P_p \times R_a \times IPP$$

where N_a is the number of risky acts per year, P_p is the proportion of risky acts done without condoms, R_a is the risk of HIV transmission per unprotected act if the partner is HIV+, and IPP is the proportion of all acts done with HIV+ partners. My hypothesis is that, for Fast Lane gay men, the gradual increase in IPP more than compensates for any decreases in N_a and P_p. So, even though people behave more cautiously as they age, they nonetheless get infected more. And the annual HIV incidence in the gay male population cohorts– assuming a 25%/75% split between Fast Lane and Not-Fast Lane– changes very little with aging, from about 7 per 1,000 at age 20 to 6 per 1,000 at age 45. This crude model thus envisions an STD which indeed affects older people as much as younger. But as Rotello argues, this would change to the degree Fast Lane culture is suppressed.

Testing the Hypothesis. Conduct a longitudinal study of gay men or IDUs, following the risky practices and seroconversion rates of a large sample throughout their young adulthood.

(3) Save Many Trees But Lose the Forest: The Paradox of Drug Treatment

Background. From the perspective of drug treatment programs and their clients, a lot of good is obviously being done. Whether it's methadone maintenance, residential treatment, or outpatient drug-free, many success stories can be cited. The turnaround in people's lives is beautiful and poignant. Moreover, it's cost-effective: with as few as 20 true success stories in a million-dollar program, the program will reach its "quota" and pay for itself– and many programs can document many times their "quota".

Hypothesis. The paradox is that, from society's point of view, all this good work is just a drop in the bucket– or, more precisely, a pint in a gallon. The problem is the scale of drug treatment: there needs to be about eight times as much. It's not just that there are chronically too few slots for "treatment on demand", but also that the treatment programs mostly fall woefully short of providing the thoroughgoing help (better housing conditions, psychotherapy, couples therapy, jobs) that people need. So from the user's point of view, a drug treatment program is merely an occasional comfort station along a decades-long career path of addiction.

Testing the Hypothesis. Obtain a random sample of citizens in their 50s who are in recovery (i.e., abstinent) after prolonged addiction. Then do in-depth interviews around the question, "What were the things that helped you begin a life in recovery?" If "treatment programs" comprise only 10% or 15% of the aggregate list of things, my hypothesis is essentially proven.

A Radical Suggestion. Obviously local, state and Federal governments should "invest" many times more in treatment, because the return on investment will be huge. San Francisco's Treatment on Demand task force strove mightily to achieve this multifold increase, as have many other well-meaning task forces.

Very little has changed. Why? The short answer is that government bodies in general lack the vision to "invest" wisely.

My radical proposal is to privatize drug treatment. Entrepreneurs would "invest" by providing the services they judge to be most cost-effective to the target populations. Return on investment would be in proportion to outcomes: the greater the decline in substance abuse (and in property crimes, joblessness, domestic violence, and other blights associated with substance abuse,) the greater the profits. One easily measured outcome would be the increase in property values in a neighborhood where drug-abuse blights disappear. Increased property values translate to increased property tax collections; that increase could be passed on to the entrepreneurs as a reward for their investment.

II.

HISTORY

All our lives, we've had to do our own cooking and cleaning. "The Servants' Century Off" predicts that the help will be back soon. "Stern-Men and Bow-Men" explains why East Coast boatmen face backwards, and West Coast boatmen forwards, in their work. Well-meaning people devise policies to reform the world, and often make things <u>worse</u> in the process; "The Institute for Policy Negation" calls for a Counter-Reformation. "Evaporation" suggests that some classes of people– burglars, speedfreaks– may gradually and quietly disappear. The "Mobutu Letter" advises the President-for-Life how he can lead a heroic counterattack against the rebels. "Correspondence" reminds America's drug czar that US policies haven't worked, and that it's time to consider legalization. "Blood on Their Hands" reflects on the only punishment ever likely to be meted out to ruling-class policymakers whose decisions cost thousands of lives or billions of dollars. "What We Have Gained" is a look at the upside of September 11th, while "What We Have Lost" is a systematic and skeptical survey of nostalgia.

In the Dedication, I imagine the world in the year 3000. It's quite possible that the majority of people in that world will be my descendants. Here's my reasoning: I assume that the Third Millennium world will have a steady population of about 9 billion, because humans keep to an average of two children per person. If we average 30 years between generations, there will be about 33 generations between now and 3000.

I have two children. If they and their descendants keep to that two-children, 30-year-generation average, then I will have about 2^{33} descendants in the year 3000. That's about 8.6 billion people. Of course, many of these 8.6 billion will "overlap" through incest among 30th cousins and suchlike; and lots of people in 3000 will somehow not have me among their 8.6 billion ancestors of the 33rd degree. But it's a fair assumption, I believe, that my genetic "spread" will be comprehensive and worldwide after a thousand years.

The Servants' Century Off

Our family's servants, along with most every other family's, have been off for most of the Twentieth Century. Around 1914 they all gave notice, declaring that they were off to be soldiers or factory workers or office workers or whatever tempting things these modern times offered. On departure, they left us a note, with saucy admonitions to the effect that we shouldn't have been so condescending, and that we should have paid better wages, and given fringe benefits. In the decades since, as we washed our own dishes and made our own beds and vacuumed our own floors, we've had ample time for sober reflection on those admonitions. We've resolved to treat our domestic help better when their century off is over, around 2010. We're glad that there will indeed *be* servants, thanks to so many of them ignoring *our* admonition to "have few children, and educate them well!"

I looked over our family records, and found to my surprise that the servants have taken a hundred years off regularly every five-and-a-half centuries. Back in the 1340s we went through the Black Death, which killed nearly half of us, servants and families alike. When that terrible plague was over, there was a serious shortage of labor, so for the first time serving people could demand *cash wages*. Not content with the shelter and food we'd provided them before, they wanted *a shilling a week* for their work! In silver! We were so shocked that it took until 1450 to recover, and finally to accede to our peoples' reasonable (and irresistible) demands.

The previous century off started in 800, when the Vikings began to loot and burn the manor houses. We approached our serving people, saying, "We'll need your help– you must take up arms and help defend the place against these bloodthirsty barbarians!" They answered, "Hell, no– we're out of here!" and fled to the inland hills. We had no choice but to do the same, so there ensued a dark century of fear, privation, and *no domestic help.*

Our family records for the early part of the Christian era are spotty, and difficult to translate from the provincial Latin of the times. Apparently, though, the whole Third Century was another hundred years off for our domestic staff. It all had to do with the competence of the emperors– in the Second Century we were well-favored with Trajan and Hadrian and Marcus Aurelius and Commodus, who gave a long sunny era of peace and prosperity. But there ensued a Third Century of thoroughly bad emperors– Caracalla (ugh!), Heliogabalus (blecch!), and Maximinus (arrrgh!), and *worse.* Amid this chaos, people fled the old villa, and didn't start trickling back until nearly 300 A.D.

In retrospect, then, a regular century off for the servants is a good thing. People have time to stretch their legs and see the world, after which of course they conclude that the old ways are best. They return with renewed devotion to their masters, and we, for our part, gain a fresh appreciation for competent domestic help. So it is with cheerful hearts that we spruce up the maids' rooms, organize the fringe benefits programs, and adapt the old lists of chores to the new household technologies. We're well-prepared for the servants' imminent return, and I think when they take off again (around the middle of the Twenty-Fifth Century, assuming they adhere to their once-every-550 years pattern) there'll be no need for admonitions.

Stern-Men and Bow-Men

(A dinnertime toast)

"**O**ur guest of honor today is Craig Lambert, out west to flog his new book, *Mind Over Water*. His book is about the art of rowing– but the watercraft he writes about are quite different from the canoes and kayaks that we see on our West Coast rivers and estuaries.

"Now, you will have noticed that Craig's boatmen are **stern-men**, that is, they face rearwards as they propel their craft. By contrast, we of the West are **bow-men**, who face forwards in our work.

"Why, Craig may rightly ask, do we Westerners give up the manifestly greater speed of a well-rowed shell where a nine-foot oar, levered against an outboard fulcrum and powered by strong thigh and back muscles, can easily yield 12 miles per hour, a third faster than the best-paddled canoe? We have three good reasons for being **bow-men**–

"First, the West is a dangerous and unsettled frontier. A boatman must keep a lookout for savage aborigines or gun-toting desperadoes in the wild landscape ahead.

"Second, there is our ornery individualism, summed up in Merriwether Lewis's motto *se quisque fulcire ipse debet* ("A man must be his own fulcrum"). The suntanned hands that hold a paddle can be both lever and fulcrum.

"Finally, the left half of our country has much more *range of altitude* than the right half, more than fourteen thousand feet compared to barely six thousand. This means the average declivity of our rivers is greater, which in turn means that boaters under Western skies must be prepared to deal with the *rapid approach of rocks*– a threat more nimbly fended off by a four-foot freeheld paddle than a nine-foot fixed oar.

"Thus are three damn good reasons for Westerners to be **bow-men**. But I should note that some Westerners are **stern-men**, and some Easterners **bow-men**. Those East Coast eight-man rowing shells usually have a ninth person– a coxswain– facing forward and steering the craft with stern determination toward some goal. Likewise, the West Coast canoe often has an attractive girl or fellow lying languidly on cushions in the front, facing sternward and admiring the muscular paddler who guides the craft. The paddler, like the cox, has his eye fixed on a goal, but in this case he's looking for a soft grassy bank where picnic delectables can be sampled and kisses stolen. Both paddler and cox are energized by testosterone, but one in an Eastern way and the other in the manner of the West...

"All this being said, we Westerners must admit an admiration of you **stern-men** for the gentle civility of your riverine culture. We suspect that this civility translates to enlightened dinnertime conversation, so we welcome you to our table!"

The Institute for Policy Negation

by Fr. Ignatius Newmeyer

I have observed that public policies, despite the good intentions with which they are conceived and executed, often leave the world *worse* off. Some arenas seem particularly prone to unintended and unhappy policy consequences:

- Welfare programs for the poor
- Military interventions
- Promoting agriculture in marginal lands
- "Improving" the lot of indigenous peoples
- Controlling substance use

I know a lot about the last of these: I've been responsible for 20 years for monitoring the level of use of illicit drugs in San Francisco. In those years, huge amounts of taxpayer money were spent to urge people to avoid drugs, to arrest dealers, to interdict drug importation, and to destroy crops on the ground. In spite of these heroic efforts, three of the four major drugs (heroin, cocaine, and "speed") now cost less on the street, and are more widely used, than in 1980. Only marijuana costs more and is used less than 20 years ago. The question naturally arises, "Would we be better off now if *no* substance use control policies had been devised and carried out?" And if we dare to think the answer might be "yes", what can we do in the future to prevent ill-fated policies from being launched?

The problem is that, in substance use as in so many other arenas, the advantage lies with those who are eager to *do something*. We Americans are persistently hopeful that our condition can be improved through planning. Our mayors, legislators, and social science faculties have a can-do attitude. So we send immigrants to plow the future Dust Bowl, we build high-rise public housing monstrosities fated for dynamiting, and we send half a million citizens to prison for no other crime than peddling feel-good substances. Always there have been doubters, but always they lacked the esprit and institutional cohesion of the boosters. But maybe, just maybe... :

My suggestion is that we create an academy dedicated to resisting policy implementation, known as the **Institute for Policy Negation**. Its Latin motto would be *Considerate Nihil Agere* ("Consider doing nothing", or alternatively, "Leave it the **** alone!") The Institute would take a Jesuit form: bright, ambitious men and women would enter a four-year advanced-level program to hone their skills in analysis, debate, and communication. Each I.P.N. graduate would become splendidly able to fudge, delay, negotiate, and compromise. They would learn the arts of organizing resistance among people affected by policy initiatives, of "questioning the need for this program," of "further study is needed." They would become masters at generating public anxiety about "hidden costs," "unintended consequences," "the loss of what we hold dear," and so forth. Most of all, each graduate would have the knack of yielding– if yield he must– with a thunderous, "I demand future accounting for the extravagant use of taxpayer dollars upon which we are about to embark!" The graduate would be individually responsible to monitor this accounting– but that role would be backed by the institutional memory of the I.P.N. to assure that the architects of failed policies, and their disciples, would be hounded by blame and ridicule *for decades* after the event.

It's likely that **Institute for Policy Negation** graduates will have a distinctive personal style not unlike Jesuits: skeptical, caustic, world-weary, but open to fleshly pleasures and laughter. That style would contrast with the earnest, optimistic, but somewhat naive personal style of the policy enthusiasts. And the enthusiasts would come to *expect* their opponents to appear ("I rise to challenge the rosy assumptions of Dr. — !") in setpiece battles as routine in 21st Century America as Democrat-Republican confrontations in the 20th Century.

I.P.N. graduates would not automatically reject all policy initiatives, yielding gracefully in many an arena– public health outreach to children, for example. But even there, there would be a tone of hesitation and skepticism.

Ideally, the **Institute for Policy Negation** should be an adjunct of Yale University. In New Haven, I.P.N. students and faculty would have the salutary experience of living amidst the evidence of countless failed social science schemes to "improve" the town and its people.

Other nations will no doubt create their own versions of the Institute– in France, an "Ecole Normale de Nonadministration", and in Britain, perhaps a Melbourne College added to the Oxford University system, wherein students could master the style of Prime Minister Melbourne:

To promise, pause, prepare, postpone
And end by letting things alone:
In short, to earn the people's pay
By doing nothing every day.

Evaporation

On occasion, a great and mighty social force will simply "evaporate" from the stage of history without ever being decisively confronted or defeated. The supreme example is Napoleon's Grand Army. This force of 600,000 men, led by the military genius who had conquered Europe, fought its way successfully to Moscow in the summer of 1812. It lingered there through September, hoping in vain that Czar Alexander would sue for peace. Leo Tolstoy, in *War and Peace,* describes what happened next:

> "After the French victory at Borodino there was no general engagement nor any that were at all serious, yet the French army ceased to exist...
>
> "There was no forage for the horses or the cattle...the peasants of the district burned their hay rather than let the French have it...
>
> "The members of what had once been an army– Napoleon himself and all his soldiers– fled without knowing whither, each concerned only to make his escape as quickly as possible from this position, of the hopelessness of which they were all more or less vaguely conscious...they all went without knowing whither or why they were going...each was thinking only of himself and of how to get away quickly and save himself."

The destruction of the Grand Army was akin to evaporation: a gradual, little-by-little process by which a huge force vanished without any sudden traumas. Tolstoy likened it to "melting away at the uniform rate of a mathematical progression." I believe a similar thing is happening in San Francisco to a social force that, while anything but grand, has nonetheless powerfully affected life in this city for decades: burglary. The class of people who commit burglaries is evaporating away, little by little, almost without anyone noticing it. Here is the evidence:

Reported Burglaries, San Francisco, 1976-2000

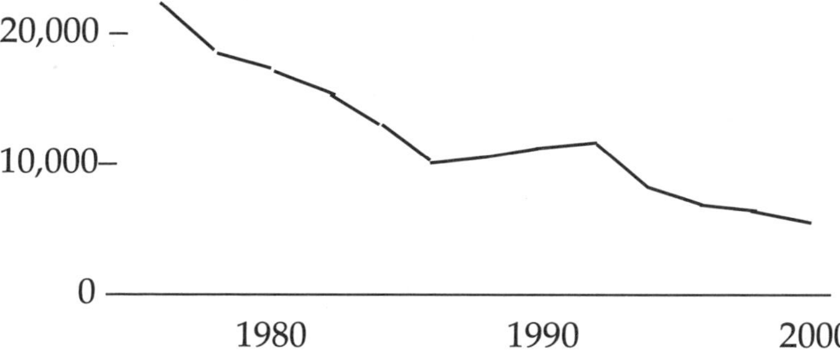

The rate of reported burglaries has fallen by *more than three-quarters* since 1976. Lest we think this unprecedented decline is an artifact of decreased reporting, or merely part of a statewide trend, here are burglary data for Vallejo, a small city 30 miles northeast of San Francisco:

Reported Burglaries, Vallejo, 1976-1998

I hypothesize that certain conditions have prevailed in San Francisco to cause rapid "evaporation" of the burglar class in the past two decades. I also hypothesize that this "evaporation" will continue, and that two other classes of people– heroin users and speed users– will also be "evaporating".

In 1812, Napoleon's army disappeared not because it was overpowered by the Russian army, but for economic reasons: there was not enough food, not enough forage, not enough shelter, not enough winter clothing. In the 1990s, people heavily into the drug scenes evaporate away from San Francisco not because of police vigilance, but for economic reasons. The main reason is that they are "downwardly mobile", experiencing disruptions such as

- job loss
- jail terms
- family instability
- evictions
- "hit the road, Jack!", i.e. female householders no longer permitting drug-using boyfriends to shack up with them

in a city where there is vastly expanded gentrification of neighborhoods, leading to

- rising property values and rents
- increased neighborhood cohesion and "vigilance"
- fewer vacant lots or buildings

Evaporation happens to burglars, speed users, and heroin users little by little. For one reason or another, they can't go back to live where they used to, and they can't get it together to find a new place to live in the incredibly competitive housing environment of San Francisco. So they leave, one by one, unnoticed, perhaps to "precipitate" nearby in Vallejo or Fremont or Daly City. The result is that San Francisco's burglary rate has plummeted, and so will its prevalence of speed users and heroin users. This phenomenon is well under way in a few other "gentrifying" cities, most notably San Jose, Manhattan, and Boston.

Endurance

In the face of this "evaporation", will the population of injection drug users in San Francisco gradually decline to zero? Or will pockets of users endure in the face of the economic factors cited above? I believe three classes of IDUs will hang on, at least for some years:

- **Bourgeois Bohemians.** "Bobos" are eloquently described in David Brooks' book, *Bobos in Paradise*. "Bobos" are able to thrive in the middle-class world of high-paying jobs, family responsibilities, homeownership, etc., while simultaneously enjoying a freewheeling, casual lifestyle. That lifestyle can include use of marijuana, ecstasy, psychedelics, perhaps even injected heroin or speed. Such "controlled" use of injected drugs is nearly invisible, because the key indicators (overdose deaths, emergency-room visits, publicly-funded treatment, arrests) rarely detect it.

- **Downwardly-Mobile Middle Class.** I've noticed that about one-third of the clients seen at Haight-Ashbury Free Clinic Detox for primary heroin problems report that they've had at least some college education. Such individuals can be described as having been on a path to middle-class status–though the majority of them were jobless by the time they entered treatment here. They are downwardly mobile: they enter adulthood with considerable assets but gradually lose them. However, it takes years for hard drug use to degrade those assets to the point where the user can no longer keep it together to stay in San Francisco.

• **The Homeless.** By simply living on the street, one avoids having to cope with the high cost of living in this city. A large number of people (estimates run as high as 14,000) are surviving in this way, and a substantial minority of them use injectable drugs at least occasionally. They are particularly at risk for HIV and HCV infection because of their living conditions. However, few of them can manage steady heroin or speed habits: injectable drugs are expensive and cash is short, and the option of cheap vodka ($4 per pint) is always available.

I predict that these three groups will dominate the IDU population by 2003, having supplanted the working-class users who had predominated among IDUs here for the past 30 years. Toward the end of this decade, I predict, the IDU population will level off at about half of the current level of 15,000. These survivors will be about equally divided among the three groups mentioned above, with the working-class user group almost completely "evaporated".

Emigration

If it's true that major parts of the target groups for HIV prevention– heroin users, speed users, perhaps sexually hyperactive youth and clubgoers as well– are emigrating from San Francisco, what about the professionals and paraprofessionals who had been providing HIV prevention services to those folks? Most of these prevention workers can remain in the city thanks to steady jobs and rent control. But they're losing their clientele. I suggest that the right thing to do is to encourage *emigration of expertise* to follow the emigrated target groups. Here are some examples of how we service providers might adapt:

• You work for the Stop AIDS Project. At the annual AIDS Update Conference, held at Brooks Hall in the Civic Center every March, you find yourself in the same room with lots of people from other parts of the Bay Area who are concerned with HIV prevention among gay men. You think, why not do a little networking to create an enlarged Stop AIDS Project, to serve the greater Bay Area rather than merely San Francisco?

• You are visiting your cousin in Vallejo. You notice that a lot of his neighbors– second-generation Filipino-Americans like yourself– are getting involved in heroin. You muse, why not set up a Twelve Step group, like the one you attend here in S.F., to help these young people recover?

• You are a Community Health Outreach Worker. Every summer you spend a couple weeks at a friend's cabin in the Sierra foothills. You notice knots of white kids hanging out in Nevada City, with the unmistakable signs of a speed scene. It occurs to you, why not do a little community health outreach among them, just as you do in San Francisco?

• You are an epidemiologist working on HIV and drug use questions. You read in the "Quarterly AIDS Surveillance Report" for June 2000 that 27,006 San Francisco residents have been diagnosed with AIDS since 1981, that 18,287 have died, and that there are 8,719 "living AIDS cases". You notice that the third figure is exactly the difference between the first and second figures, and ask yourself, "Hey— how do we know those 8,719 people are still in San Francisco? Isn't it possible that many of them moved away long ago?"

Mobutu Letter

March 25, 1997

President-for-Life Mobutu Sese Seko
Gdabolite Palace
Kinshasa, ZAIRE

Dear President Mobutu:

I read with interest of your return to Zaire, to resume the reins of power after your illness. Of course you are aware of the rebellion in the eastern part of your country, led by Mr. Laurent Kabila and aimed at overthrowing the government which was legitimately seized by you in 1965. I write with advice as to how that rebellion can be defeated.

You must keep in mind the example of the Emperor Napoleon Bonaparte, who, when pressed by the Allied advance upon Paris in 1814, rallied his people to resist. You should assemble your finest military dress uniform, red and purple with gold epaulets and trimmings, and topped with a helmet well-flared with ostrich plumes. Then you should lead your troops on horseback– it is vital that the horse be *white*– out of Kinshasha to meet the foe. The troops should be naked except for loincloths and shell necklaces, and should carry long spears. Their lightweight gear will enable them to make their way eastward along the enjungled ex-highways; rifles and grenades can be issued to them when they arrive at the front line. Of course there should be drumming, bagpiping, and the singing of stirring martial songs.

Upon engagement with the enemy, battle tactics should

include the *smart cannonade*, the *infantry envelopment*, and the *all-out cavalry charge*, this last led in person by yourself in the style of Alexander the Great. Always remember that victory goes to the army with the greatest *esprit*.

I am mindful of the pain and difficulty of an eight hundred mile horseback ride, so soon into recovery from prostate cancer. I enclose a recipe for a soothing syrup, of cocaine, morphine, and Valium® in grain alcohol. You should swallow three tablespoonfuls of this syrup whenever the pain troubles you.

In confident assurance of complete victory for your cause, I remain,

Yours sincerely,

John Newmeyer, Ph.D.
Military Historian

A Correspondence on Prohibition

December 7, 1996

Alan Leshner, Director
National Institute on Drug Abuse
Rockville, MD 20857

Dear Dr. Leshner,

At our breakfast meeting on Tuesday you quoted a sign in your office: "The definition of insanity is the repetition of unsuccessful behavior." Immediately I (and several others present) thought of the supreme example of unsuccessful behavior: the Nation's prohibition policies. We would love to know whether those policies are sometimes in your mind, too, when you look at your sign.

It would be a worthy project for NIDA to produce a consensus operational definition of "unsuccessful", so that we can objectively measure the success of our magnificent, costly drugs prohibition experiment. To find a clear negative outcome would enable the Nation, at last, seriously to consider the most obvious alternative behavior, recently summarized by *The Economist* in four words: "Legalize, regulate, tax, discourage." Of course, we might even then choose to persist in the unrewarded behavior, in which case we would be well served by historians to chronicle our collective "insanity".

Sincerely,

John Newmeyer, Ph.D.

******

December 20, 1996

Alan Leshner, Director
National Institute on Drug Abuse
Rockville, MD 20857

Dear Dr. Leshner,

Thank you for your thoughtful and articulate letter of December 16th.

You are correct that we dissenters have yet to prove our case. We have not fully documented the costs of prohibition, particularly

- the criminalization of huge numbers of Americans;
- the overburdening of courts and prisons;
- the reduction of quality of life and property values in our cities;
- the absence of potential revenues from sin taxes;
- the lack of regulatory limits on the potency, purity, and marketing of drugs; and
- the huge transfer of wealth to some rather nasty people.

Adequate documentation may take years, even decades, during which time documentation of the *benefits* of prohibition may also be pursued: worthy tasks to which to devote our professional lives, both at NIDA and out in the field. I'm reminded of Ho Chi Minh's comment that the ending of Western domination of Vietnam might require 100 years of struggle.

I remain interested in your private take on the War on Drugs: absolutely certain it must be continued, or open to consider alternatives?

Best wishes,

John Newmeyer

******

January 1, 1997

Dear Alan,

Thanks very much for your letter of the 25th, relating the private views of yourself, Secretary Shalala, and Vice President Gore on the prohibition debate. I was surprised, but not astounded, by what I read.

Of course, you have my word of honor that I will keep the contents of your letter in the <u>strictest</u> confidence.

Warmly,

John

Blood on Their Hands: The Judgment of History

A lower-class thief steals a thousand dollars worth of property, and– if caught and convicted three times for such theft– is punished by 25 years in a nasty and brutal penitentiary.

A middle-class savings and loan exploiter defrauds a million dollars from the depositors, and– if caught at it and very unlucky– is punished by a few years in a minimum-security prison.

But what punishment awaits a ruling-class policymaker, whose bad decisions cost the taxpaying public a billion dollars– or thousands of human lives?

Usually, *none whatsoever*. A sterling example is General Douglas Haig, who commanded British armies in the murderous trench warfare of World War One. After the War, he was raised to the peerage and given a grant of £100,000; upon his death in 1928, he was accorded national tributes to his memory at Westminster Abbey.

Another example is Robert McNamara, the chief architect of the U.S. role in the Vietnam War. Despite doubts that (as he later admitted) began in 1965, he carried on the War with increased intensity, only resigning late in 1967 after billions more dollars and thousands more lives had been squandered. He went on to prestigious employment running the World Bank, and then a comfortable retirement.

The only "punishment" for Haig and McNamara and their ilk is the savage judgment of History. Of Haig the official view (*Encyclopedia Britannica,* 1974) now reads, "...his strategies of attrition (tautly summarized as 'kill more Germans') resulted in enormous numbers of British casualties but little immediate gain in 1916-17." An even more caustic view of McNamara is gradually emerging in the long-term history of the Vietnam War era.

It is embittering to realize that the egregious decisionmakers who stymied needle exchange and bleach-and-teach for so long– I am resisting the temptation to name names here– will enjoy lives like Haig's and McNamara's. They'll keep their jobs, and even be promoted or re-elected.

At least we are beginning to write the shameful history of the early years of the war against HIV. Our revenge, for what it's worth, will be History's judgment, summarized in the enduring metaphor of "blood on their hands."

What We Have Gained

The catastrophe of September 11th cost thousands of lives and billions of dollars. That day changed our society in some unpleasant ways, not least of which is the greater inconvenience of air travel. However, we have coped with the tragedy in some heartening ways, among which I cite these:

(1) **People are nicer to acquaintances and strangers.** This country became a palpably kinder place after September 11th. Even drivers seem to evince more "road grace" than "road rage". This quality is easier to notice if one turns off the TV and ignores the newspapers.
Prediction: There will be lower rates of violent crimes in September/October 2001 than in September/October 2000.

(2) **People have a deeper relationship with their friends and loved ones.** "...no one exists alone/ hunger allows no choice/ to the citizen or the police/ we must love one another or die" wrote W.H. Auden at the outbreak of World War II. Or, as E.M. Forster advised, "only connect!" Our renewed sense of life's fragility has also revitalized the ways we treasure those who are dear.

(3) **A little less materialism is good for us.** Our stock portfolios are emptier, but our churches and– much more important– our caring hearts are fuller. After the greed and self-absorption of the late 1990s, we should welcome this change.

(4) **Though the terrorists have won a tactical victory, they have suffered a strategic defeat.** Our enemies don't seem to have learned that their only real hope is an America divided and purposeless. Atrocities and sneak attacks– sinking neu-

tral ships in 1917, bombing Pearl Harbor in 1941, viciously attacking South Korea in 1950– serve to awaken and give purpose to the sleeping American giant.

(5) **Hijackers will henceforth always face revolt by the passengers.** Such a revolt on United Flight 93 thwarted that plane's hijackers. This will add to the challenge of potential hijackers, who also will have to deal with well-locked pilot's cabins and armed personnel.
Prediction**:** There will be zero hijackings in the United States in the next 12 months.

(6) **Patriotic Arab-Americans.** The vast majority of Arab-Americans are happy to be in this country and are horrified at the events of September 11. They will be valuable as a source of information. Whenever any terrorist cell recruits a new member, it just might bring in a double agent.
Prediction: From December 2001 onward, the majority of arrests of suspected terrorists will result from infiltrators of their own kind.

(7) **"Human intelligence" gains at the expense of technological fixes.** The September 11 attacks could not have been prevented by missile defense systems or other forms of military high technology. They *could* have been prevented by better intelligence about what certain people were saying and doing. This lesson will not be lost, here and in the rest of the world. Nearly everyone has something to gain from passing on information about suspected terrorist activities. We only need to learn to reward the right information in the right manner.

(8) **We're more aware of the world than in any previous conflict.** A higher proportion of Americans has traveled abroad than at any time in our history. In particular, many

have seen the Third World and the effects that U.S. economic hegemony had had in it; others have "voyaged" there by Internet chat rooms or by reading of informed commentary. This results in an awareness on the part of some– not all, nor even most– Americans of the urgent need to change the conditions which breed the terrorist mentality. Perhaps we'll apply our wealth and creative energy toward ways to promote hope and opportunity rather than despair and rage, in those Palestinian and Afghan refugee camps.
<u>Prediction</u>: By the end of 2001, most college-educated Americans will have a nuanced understanding of what motivates terrorists.

--September 18, 2001

What We Have Lost

People of a certain age often wax nostalgic about "the way things were." Such nostalgia has been observed at least as far back as the Roman poet Ovid. If human society had been losing good things for so many generations, by the first half of the 20th Century nearly everything of value should have disappeared. But that era seemed fine enough to those who lived in it– so I thought I'd take a closer look at nostalgia for those particular old days.

I contacted fourteen people[1] whom I respected as keen observers, and who lived part of their lives before 1950. I asked them to list items of nostalgia– "what we have lost." Seventy-two Nostalgia Items were nominated. They fell into three groups of roughly equal size:

(A) What we were– Abilities, manners, ways of acting that existed a generation or two ago but less so (or not at all) now.

(B) What we had– Goods and services that could be had a generation or two ago, but less so (or not at all) now.

(C) Markers of the good old days– Things of lesser importance than (A) and (B), but which nonetheless are sweet reminders of a world that is gone.

---

1 For valuable recommendations of Nostalgia Items, and for general guidance on this essay, I am indebted to Randy Delehanty, Adam Donovan, Richard Ferguson, Michael Hathaway, Bryan Hemming, Richard Hilkert, Fred Hirth, Fred Hudson, Stuart Loomis, John Pence, Peter Pursley, Fred Sonenburg, Philip Fay Stevenson, and George Timson.

A. What we were

1. Neighbors and relatives who grow fruits and vegetables.
2. Fixing broken things ourselves, and making many of the everyday things we need.
3. Hitchhiking as a good way to travel.
4. Men's hats and the associated etiquette.
5. Good public schools, where you get to grade 12 with more than half of the same classmates as in kindergarten.
6. Two parents for every kid.
7. Dressing up for train or air travel.
8. Maypoles on May Day.
9. Dressing appropriately for the opera, the symphony, and other cultural events.
10. Guilt-free enjoyment of certain "bad" foods.
11. Family and friends singing around the piano.
12. Settin' on the front porch on warm evenings.
13. Weekend parties at country houses.
14. Reticence and circumspection in public romancing.
15. Leisurely travel by auto to marvel at the great outdoors.
16. Leaving the front door and the car unlocked.
17. Extended family gatherings.
18. Meals at home, together around the dining table.
19. Genuine experience of leisure time.
20. A sense of neighborhood and community.
21. Courteous drivers.
22. Public officials we can respect and trust.
23. Letting the kids out to play in the neighborhood.
24. Being properly addressed by strangers at stores, banks, offices, etc.

B. What we had

1. Silver and gold coins in circulation.
2. Home delivery of fresh dairy products, especially milk bottles with cream at the top.
3. Doctors' house calls.
4. Codeine syrup for *real* relief of coughs.
5. Saturday matinee broadcasts of the Met.
6. Neighborhood produce trucks.
7. Live-in help.
8. Grand movie houses.
9. Gentlemen's clubs.
10. Saturday matinees for the kids.
11. Drive-in movies.
12. Diners.
13. Radio dramas and comedies.
14. Games without violence or weapons.
15. Children's books with illustrations that were works of art (e.g., N.C. Wyeth).
16. Skinny-dipping at the swimming hole.
17. Farm-fresh foods, such as corn on the cob, real tomatoes, and real strawberries.
18. Train stations in small towns.
19. *Grand luxe* train travel.
20. More local businesses, fewer franchises.
21. Foreign travel by ship, not plane.
22. Good dance music from popular singers and groups.
23. Variety shows.
24. Small, quality bookstores.
25. Well-paved and maintained streets.
26. Lively downtowns.

C. Markers of the good old days

1. Rumble seats and running boards.
2. Mail twice a day at Christmastime.
3. Handwritten missives on good stationery.
4. Named telephone prefixes.
5. Abalone.
6. Operator-assisted calls.
7. Absence of phone solicitations.
8. Door-to-door sales (encyclopedias, sewing machines, brushes, etc.)
9. Good Humor ice cream trucks.
10. Paperboys crying "Extra!"
11. Packard cars.
12. Burma Shave ads.
13. Autumn-leaf bonfires and roasted potatoes in the driveway.
14. Short subjects at the movies.
15. Nuns in habits, and in pairs.
16. The circus parade.
17. Toys of metal rather than plastic.
18. Prepaid return postage for bills.
19. Gas station attendants and free maps.
20. Soda jerks.
21. Tramps and hoboes instead of "homeless".
22. Woodies.

I think there are six important things to say about these lists. First, by no means are all of the Nostalgia Items "gone". Many of them are still with us in abundance; others can be found if we just know where to look; still others are with us in slightly modified forms. I've listed the items within each of the three categories in approximate descending order as to how truly they are "gone". Thus, B.1 through B.5 have indeed vanished, but B.6 through B.12 can still be found with a little diligence.

Second, it's obvious to me that we have a lot of control over whether things are "gone" or not. This control is expressed in the way we structure our family life (items 6, 11, 12, 16, 17, 18, and 23 in category A) and the manners we adopt and seek out in those we choose as our friends (items 7, 9, 13, and 20 in category A.)

Third, a great deal of "what we have lost" comes down to class and place of residence: *then* we were gentlemen living in small cities or towns; *now* we're men living in big cities without manners or style. But, again, we have the power to change this: why not live in places like Napa or Vallejo or Laguna Beach and why not comport ourselves like gentlemen [ladies] and seek like company?

Fourth, the rate of loss has varied over the past sixty years. I analyzed the proportion of loss of each of the 72 Nostalgia Items, to see how much could be attributed to each of three 20-year periods: 1940-1960, 1960-1980, and 1980-2000. I found that roughly two-fifths of the loss occurred in 1940-1960, about half in 1960-1980, and *barely one-tenth* since 1980. It seems that the rate of loss of things of value is decelerating– though it's possible we haven't yet noted some recent disappearances.

Fifth, the changes over time are different for the three Nostagia Item groups. Much of Group B ("what we had") and especially Group C ("markers of the good old days") had come into being only in the last 100 or 150 years:

Number of Items Extant in:

	1850	1900	1940
Group A	22	22	24
Group B	16	19	26
Group C	9	12	22
All Groups	47	53	72

It seems that much of our nostagia is associated with automobiles, radio, and movies– things unknown to Victorians. If there has been a loss of long-extant things of value, they are mostly of Group A, "what we were".

Finally, what about what we have *gained* in the past half-century? What about the children of 2000 who will know these new things and will eventually have just as much nostalgia for them as we have for the things of 1950? To say nothing of the things that have really, really made our lives a lot better:

- American women can live their lives more freely and can go further in the workplace.
- ditto, for African-Americans.
- ditto, for other racial minorities.
- ditto, for gay and lesbian Americans.
- The quality and variety of restaurants are vastly improved.
- ditto, for American wines.
- Personal computers, fax machines, and cell phones are wonderful conveniences, if occasionally pesky.
- Penicillin and other antibiotics cure some formerly-nasty diseases.
- Even if we don't travel in style, it's nice to be able to

get to Europe or Asia so quickly.

- Plus an enormous amount of excellent music, movies, books, and even (dare I say it?) television programming

My conclusion is this: we are probably creating things worthy of nostalgia as fast as we are losing them; much of what we think we've lost can still be found; and a great deal depends upon how, where, and with whom we choose to live our lives.

III.

CLASS

"Old Money" helps you to know if your vintage has reached maturity– or if sufficient time has passed for the fundamental crime to be forgotten. "Hereditary Upper Class" asks whether America has an aristocracy, and if so, will it endure? "Climbing Beacon Hill" notes that when you renovate a house, you symbolically reexperience your own upward social mobility. "Ten Commandments" is advice from Cato the Cynic to a ruling class that desires to stay on top. The richer you are, the longer the perspective you have on life; "Poor Day, Rich Life" examines this phenomenon in household shopping, substance use, and HIV treatment. "AIDS and Class" looks at the role of class in the way AIDS is experienced. "Sick and Poor, Sick and Rich" enumerates the many, many reasons why it's tougher to face a disease if you're poor than if you're rich.

**Those Who Don't Fit In:
A Two-Dimensional Diagram**

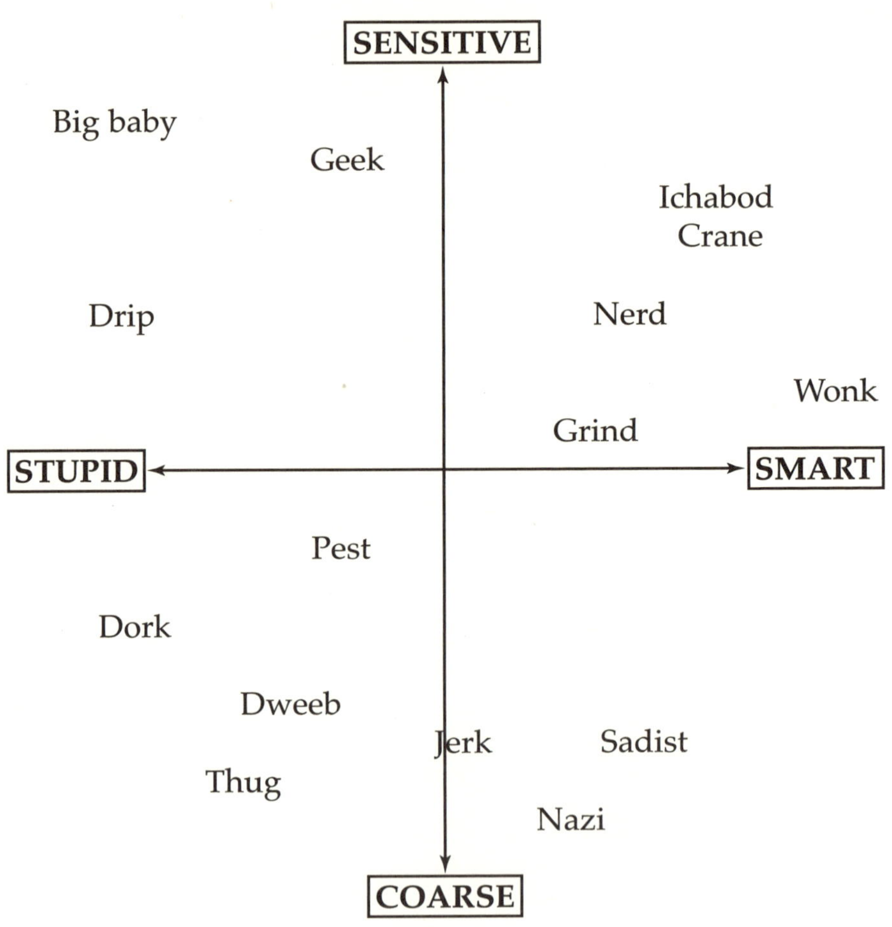

How to Tell if You're "Old Money"

- You use "summer" and "winter" as verbs.
- Among the group at lunch, conversation slides from English to French to Italian and back to English without anyone noticing.
- A trip to Europe means staying at friends' houses rather than hotels– houses often larger, older, and with better service than most hotels.
- "One doesn't do anything, but it's nice of you to ask."
- You can't recall which of your studs and things belonged to father, which to grandfather, and which to great-grandfather.
- On meeting someone from another American city, you muse, "hmmm— does our family own anything there?" as a conversation opener.
- You recall the French Revolution as an inconvenient, dangerous, and thoroughly tiresome time.
- You have substantial assets and bank accounts that you've simply forgotten about.
- On the subject of United States Senators, you think, "let's see, which ones have I met..."
- You think of money not as salary and income, but as assets and revenues.

- You look up information about your ancestors in the encyclopedia or a history textbook.
- Very little of your furniture and clothes was bought in the past ten years, and much of it not even during your lifetime.

Toward an Hereditary Upper Class

These days, the United States hasn't much of an hereditary aristocracy. Oh, we made a brave start– chronicled by Edith Wharton and Henry James– but where are those families now? Most have dissipated, thanks to divorce, profligate children, ruinous taxes, the Great Depression, etc. Is there any chance for a revival in the new century?

As I see it, seven conditions are required to create an enduring upper class in America. The current absence, or rarity, of these seven conditions goes far to explaining why there isn't such a class at present:

(1) A Family Talent. To justify aristocracy, a class must devote itself to the principle of *aristos*, the best. The upper class, family by family, must create things of value to our civilization and share them generously and tirelessly with the rest of us. This is the *sine qua non* of these seven conditions. Without it, it's not worth it: the rich would merely be ordinary people with a lot of money— might as well give up and allow the ill-used wealth to be taxed away.

With it, though— when the *aristos* principle is applied in concert with wealth and breeding and education— good things can happen. Being free from the tiresome daily business of earning a living can enable one to focus on creative work of all sorts. Of course the upper class is not the prime cause, nor even a major factor, in manifesting a civilization; but they can at least be well aware of what civilization is, and keen to *do their bit.*

It's too much to expect that a family manifest the best in everything, though of course they should have a sharp eye for it. Instead, each family should undertake to be the best at some one thing: style, music, parties, interior design, politics, winemaking, or– most desirable of all– writing.

(2) Elimination of the Death Tax. Wealth is neither necessary nor sufficient for an enduring aristocracy, but oh my, it does help. The great problem is that the wealth created by one generation is taxed twice: when it is earned, and when it is passed to the next generation. The second of these taxes is especially pernicious, not only because of the size of the bite– Federal and State taxes will take 50% to 60% of everything beyond the first million of an estate– but because government wants its money *right now.* When most of the wealth of a family is concentrated in one or two major assets– a business, a ranch, a great house– those assets may need to be sold at a low price to raise the cash for the taxes. The best reason for eliminating inheritance taxes is to keep the "family place" (see below) in the family's hands.

(3) Reconceiving Marriage. At least 40% of American marriages end in divorce. This is catastrophic to hopes to build an hereditary upper class, both because the estate is cut to pieces in the dissolution, and because children lose a sense of "family". We need to reconceive marriage as taking two distinct forms: as a love-bond between two people, or as a foundation for children and a family. The latter, "family-foundation" form should consist of a sacred vow to a partnership of childrearing, and to the integrity of the estate that those children will inherit. If the couple find that they do indeed love and cherish one another until death parts them, so much the better– but that *should not be part of the family-foundation vow.* Better a hundred mistresses or lovers than one divorce...

As the elimination of the Death Tax could be the Republican contribution to the great work of creating an American aristocracy, reconceiving marriage could be the Democrats' contribution: the former have proven fierce opponents of taxes, and the latter are open to rethinking what "marriage" means.

(4) A Sense of Place. Americans move too much. As Wallace Stegner put it, too many of us are "Boomers", shifting from one place to the next in search of that gold strike, that Big Rock Candy Mountain. Those who hope to create an inherited estate need to be "Stickers", whose first generation finds and buys its "family place", which later generations improve, love with all their hearts, and hang onto for dear life. This family place need not be grand– it can be a clapboard house in Appalachia, or a funky old ranch in Colorado, or a ramshackle lakeside retreat in Vermont– but it must be a *thing of value* which the years treat kindly.

(5) Schools for Gilded Youth. The obvious purpose of schooling is to help the children master the skills of the elite: wise use of wealth, management of staffs, elegant use of language, knowledge of history, appreciation of the arts, and so forth. All well and good– but the *real* purpose is to enable the forming of lifelong friendships that sustain class solidarity. For all of this, fine schools are needed. Most such schools are private, but there is ample opportunity for worthwhile public schools in areas where the upper class concentrates.

(6) Health. Physical health is vital; many family members should live into their eighties and beyond, to sustain a living bond across generations. Mental, emotional, and moral health are just as essential. The 20th Century left a legacy of powerful methods to restore those sorts of health– family counseling, Twelve Step, Outward Bound, Prozac. These should be applied as needed, with the will to be realistic about failure to recover health: a family shouldn't hesitate to disinherit its fools, liars, gamblers, drunkards, and nutcases.

(7) A Paterfamilias. The history of Western nations since 1789 shows that lethal *external* challenges to inherited wealth arise about three times every two centuries. The main job of the paterfamilias (or materfamilias) is to beware of such challenges, and ensure that the family's asset base is maintained and expanded. Each generation, the family fortunes must be entrusted to someone who is smart about maintaining ownership of wealth, and diversifying across many forms (businesses, bonds, equities, cash, collectibles, real estate) and across borders.

The greatest *internal* challenges to inherited wealth arise from too much division among heirs, and from the folly of those heirs. These challenges are met by a willingness to disinherit foolish or profligate children, and a commitment to primogeniture if there are too many competent children for too little wealth.

Naturally there is the danger that the paterfamilias might be an egotistical madman– a Howard Hughes or a Herbert Haft. Each family needs to create its own sort of checks and balances to deal with this danger.

* * * * * * *

This list of seven consists of six items about preserving an upper class, plus one about justifying its existence. When I speculate about the hopes for an upper class in the new century, I realize that the absence of the one may obviate any success with the other six. It is an old story in this country, and I believe it will be repeated this time: tomorrow's rich will once again be too vulgar, too selfish, too culturally numb, to create an aristocracy worthy of the name. They will be Millionaires Next Door[1]: uninteresting people who happen to have lots of money.

Perhaps, though, the competitive streak of the American rich will be aroused. Perhaps they will read the history of other peoples at the peak of their economic power– the Italians in the Renaissance, the Dutch in the 17th Century, the English in the late 19th Century– and marvel at the cultural flourishing of the rich in those eras. Perhaps they will think, "Hey– we're Americans! We can do better!" And perhaps they will make a try, family by family, at outdoing the Medicis, the de Ruyters, and the Balfours at the great game of creating a civilization.

---

1 T. Stanley and W. Danko, in *The Millionaire Next Door: The Surprising Secrets of America's Wealthy* (1996), describe at great length how very frugal, ordinary, and "middle class" are the lives of today's rich. Tellingly, they speak of this lifestyle as if it were a good thing...

Climbing Beacon Hill

My friend Tony lives on Brimmer Street, where Boston's Beacon Hill meets the Charles River shoreline. During my visit with him last month, we were inspired to examine a handsome old brick building nearby that was beginning renovation. The crew were on their lunch break, and the foreman kindly assented to our request to have a look around.

We climbed all through the building, amazed by what we saw: the demolition crew had fully gutted the place, and there remained little more than five levels of floor-joists joined together by rickety stairways, all of it resting wetly on scores of pilings which, in 1870, had created the original foundation in the shoreline mudflats. Even more amazing was the foreman's report that the new owner had paid a million dollars for the property, and intended to spend another million on a complete reconstruction. We marveled at the sight: a million bucks already, to get little more than an 18′ x 60′ space bounded by four brick walls towering fifty feet into the Boston sky.

I thought about the months of hard work ahead to turn this dusty shell into a fine residence, and realized that the Owner would come to know the wisdom of the old saying, **"renovation recapitulates rising"**. That is, in the several steps of creating a new home on this site, he will symbolically re-experience the stages by which a young man rises in the world, from a humble origin up through the middle class to patrician heights. At each stage of the renovation project, the Owner will work with people who will take him a step higher in the socioeconomic hierarchy, something like this:

- He'll start with the demolition crew, in this case eight unskilled but strong African-American fellows from Roxbury. The work will be dirty and dangerous, the humor coarse but brotherly.

- Next will come the construction crew, most likely semiskilled Irish-Americans from South Boston. They'll do the rough framing and dry-walling, and put in the flooring and roofing.

- Then it will be time for the skilled trades– licensed plumbers and electricians, and master cabinetmakers and metalworkers. I imagine family men from places like Waltham, of Italian or Irish ancestry, doing this phase of the work. Wages will be good, but hands will be callused, collars will be blue, and airs will be conspicuous by their absence.

- By now the residence will be fully constructed and ready for the involvement of middle-class skills, namely those of an interior decorator. I visualize a nicely-dressed young man, recently graduated from the Rhode Island School of Design. Colors and fabrics will be selected, windows and floors will be "treated", fashionable (and pricey) furniture will be bought, lighting will be arranged *just so.*

- Finally comes the time to install art on the walls, and books in the library, to reflect the Owner's taste and cultivation. The Owner, realizing that he is no more capable of this task than he would have been as electrician, or carpenter, or decorator– hey, who had time to learn such things when it's taken 20 years of seven-day workweeks with no vacations to make his company what it is today, twelve branches all through New England and now expanding nationwide?– once again hires the help he needs. Thus does a Harvard man, an expert in Renaissance studies, motor in from West Newton to tour the newly-done residence and dictate his *very pricey* selections for wall and bookshelf.

• At last the place will be ready for its formal dedication. And what a place– five elegant floors, a formal dining room, a walnut-paneled library, three handsome bedrooms, four bathrooms with marble *for days*. Veritably a mansion, of a piece with other Beacon Hill edifices handed down in Brahmin families of ancient lineage and wealth. Surely the Owner, whose fortune resulted from the same kind of grit and energy as the Brahmins', belongs in this exalted place; even if he still has many rough edges, surely just living in this splendid home will smooth them over. A brilliant housewarming, graced by the right guest of honor, is just the thing to signal to the world that the Owner is ready to claim patrician status. With the intervention of his Harvard consultant, the proper introductions are made, and the elegant Mrs. Isabel Saltonstall Lowell is seen to walk those few score steps down from Louisburg Square to bless the house of her new neighbor. She finds the Owner's friends and associates an odd bunch, but converses with them well enough ("Why– one doesn't <u>do</u> anything, young man, but it's nice of you to ask...") and the housewarming is a success.

Thus will the Owner do his great work, with each step cleaner and more elegant than the last, just as his own life has been grander and finer at each step of his rise in the world. Of course the people he works with will see the project in their own ways: the demolition men and the construction crew will wonder why the hell such strong old walls were pulled down to be replaced with flimsy modern materials ("they don't build 'em like they used to"); Mrs. Lowell will agree, as the house had seemed lovely enough when she was last here forty years ago, as a schoolgirl visiting her friend who now lives in Paris and writes for *The New Yorker;* but the electricians and the plumbers and the decorator will think the changes are just fine, as one should always take advantage of the new technologies and fashions. As for the cabinetmakers and the metalworkers, they know they can equal the Victorian craftsmanship that was torn out, if only the Owner will recognize that *many hours of labor* (at $74/hour plus benefits plus State and Federal taxes) will be needed.

The Owner will have his own misgivings. With the demolition and the construction crews, he'll have many a jolly interchange, as between plain hardworking men and a boss who appreciates competent help when he sees it. But the Owner will notice, as his project "rises", that he feels a little more uncomfortable and out of his depth at each new step; and he gets the feeling that neither Mrs. Lowell nor the Harvard man will ever be inviting him to visit *their* homes, and he also senses that even if he were invited to the decorator's South End condo, it would be for the wrong reason. Yet Renovation Recapitulates Rising has its own inner energy, and the process moves inexorably upward...

But maybe not– maybe instead, the Owner will have thoughts along the lines of, "Dammit, a guy just wants to have fun!" Maybe some airy phrase of the decorator ("...those walls could do with a little fauxing to set off the window treatments...") will detonate an epiphany in the Owner's mind, and he will decide to *halt the whole process right there.* The lithe young fellow will be packed off back to the South End, all thoughts of Harvard art consultants and Brahmin bluebloods will be set aside, and a few trips to Home Depot in a borrowed pickup will finish the job. Then the Owner will chill a case of Rolling Rock, invite over his new-made friends from Roxbury and South Boston and Waltham, order some pizzas, turn on the Red Sox game, and settle in for a robust evening of laughter and camaraderie.

* * * * * *

Of course the adventures of the Owner are a metaphor for the larger drama of millions of owners engaged in renovating the domestic architecture of this continent, shabby after twelve millennia of unambitious Native American stewardship, a Great Depression, and years of postwar urban decay. We should pause and wonder at the results to date, which speak so little of gourmet kitchens and paneled libraries and so much of pizzas and televised sports events. We should wonder why the houses of Iowa farmers are so dull when compared to those of the English landed gentry, when the former are richer by far both in acres and in cash. And we should wonder why the richest nation the world has ever known creates a hundred houses direct from Home Depot for every one worthy of *Architectural Digest*. Perhaps if we reflect upon just what that Boston Owner believes "fun" to mean, and upon the American education that led to that belief, we will have our answer...

Ten Commandments for a Ruling Class Which Desires to Endure

by Cato the Cynic

(1) Maintain ownership of sources of income generation (a.k.a. "means of production"). Diversify that ownership– across businesses, bonds, equities, cash, collectibles, real estate; and across borders.

(2) Promote any form of flat tax; discourage any form of inheritance or property tax.

(3) Have few children, and give them superb educations.

(4) Encourage the plebeians to have many children, and give them bread and circuses (a.k.a. TV entertainment.)

(5) Co-opt talented plebeians into your class. Encourage some of them to display their new wealth ostentatiously, to distract the envy of the proletariat.

(6) Regard marriage as a serious lifetime commitment– to a business partnership between two powerful families. Do whatever is necessary to sustain that partnership; regard love as a happy bonus. Better a hundred mistresses or lovers than one divorce.

(7) Practice primogeniture, but do not hesitate to disinherit your eldest if he turns out to be a gambler, a drunkard, or a fool.

(8) Train your younger sons for key roles in maintaining

the social order– the Church, the Army, finance, law, Civil Service, etc.

(9) Sexually, sons may do as they please but should not talk about it. Daughters must be chaste and monogamous until heirs are produced, after which they may do as they please but not talk about it.

(10) Teach history well to your class, and badly to the plebeians. If the plebeians begin to get wise to the social order, distract them by fomenting divisions between different races, ethnic groups, and sexual orientations.

Poor Day, Rich Life

If you're unskilled or semi-skilled in this country, you're generally paid by the hour– e.g., $5.15/hour to serve hamburgers at McDonald's. If you have middle-class skills, you're paid by the month or year– e.g., $39,000/year to teach high school in San Francisco. But if you're lucky enough to be born into the upper class, you'll be "paid" once in your life, namely when you inherit a trust fund or estate of some millions of dollars of stocks, bonds, real estate, and other assets.

Parallel to the time frames by which one is "paid" are the time frames with which life is viewed. For a truly poor person, life is coped with day by day. A middle-class person has the means to think further ahead: to next summer's vacation, or a down payment for a house. But a truly rich person, being freed from day-to-day or even year-to-year financial anxieties, can plan a whole lifetime with the assurance of prosperity; the goal is to assure similar prosperity for grandchildren and great-grandchildren. Thus, the poor live and plan by the day, and the rich, by the lifetime.

"Present value" is a way to gauge how real the future is in a person's time frame. One is asked to name the smallest value of X in, "Would you rather have X dollars now or $1,000 guaranteed in one year?" Here are some likely "present values" of X, by socioeconomic class:

Rich	$910
Middle-class	$850
Working poor	$250
Homeless	$ 20

Poor Retail, Rich Wholesale– Or, Why So Many BMWs in Costco's Lot?

There are myriad ways in which the "Poor Day, Rich Life" theme manifests itself in modern American life. Among the most striking is the buying of everyday groceries. Often the rich pay less for these needs than the poor. The best prices for groceries are found at Costco or Price Club or suchlike. But an amazingly high proportion of shoppers at wholesale outlets drive luxury cars: in one recent visit to Costco, I counted 4 Cadillacs, 3 BMWs, 3 Lexuses, 2 Land Rovers, 2 Volvos, 2 Infinitis, 2 Integras, and a Mercedes– about one-fifth of all the cars in the parking area! I wrote down Costco's prices of some basic grocery items. Later I went to the Safeway on Noriega in the middle-class Sunset district to examine prices for the same items; in that parking lot, about one in eight cars were luxury models. Finally I went to a corner grocery store in the low-income Bayview district to check on prices; there were no luxury cars to be seen at all, and neither a Safeway nor a Costco within miles. Here's what I found:

	Costco	Safeway	Corner Store
Milk	\$4.25/2 gal. (\$.53/quart)	\$3.79/gallon (\$.95/quart)	\$1.19/quart
Bread	\$2.65 for 2 big loaves (\$.66/lb.)	\$1.65 for a 24-oz. loaf (\$1.10/lb.)	\$1.89 for a 24-oz. loaf (\$1.26/lb.)
Cheerios	\$5.65/35 oz. (\$.18/oz.)	\$4.99/20 oz. (\$.25/oz.)	\$3.99/10 oz. (\$.40/oz.)

Orange Juice (frozen)	$6.15 for 6 16 oz. cans ($.06/oz.)	$1.69/16 oz. ($.11/oz.)	$1.59/12 oz. ($.13/oz.)
Cheese (cheddar)	$2.35/lb.	$2.79/lb.	$3.59/lb.
Corn (frozen)	$4.79/5 lbs. ($.96/lb.)	$2.29/2 lbs. ($1.15/lb.)	$ .89/10 oz. ($1.42/lb.)

I imagined shopping for a household of four, whose daily consumption totals one quart of milk, 12 oz. of bread, 4 oz. of Cheerios, 8 oz. of frozen orange juice, 4 oz. of cheese, and 10 oz. of corn. In a month, this is what would be spent at the three places:

Costco	$101
Safeway	$151
Corner store	$197

The difference is enormous: the rich person shopping at Costco pays barely *half* of what the poor person shopping at the local Bayview store pays. Of course, the poor can and do shop at Costco. But consider the impediments: a buyer has to obtain a Costco club membership, and needs a long view on household needs, a vehicle to get to the outlet, sufficient room in the household for storage, and a few hundred dollars of ready money, to make the trip worthwhile.

We've always known that "you get a better deal at wholesale." The surprising part is how much better a deal, and how the rich are likelier than the poor to take advantage.

How does "poor retail, rich wholesale" apply to substance use? Or to fighting HIV disease? Rather differently, it seems:

The Poor Crackster, The Rich Cocainist

What is true for basic groceries is also true for drugs and alcohol. Do you love premium scotch whiskey? Vodka? Beer? Cigarettes? Here's what you'd pay at the three stores:

	Costco	Safeway	Corner Store
Johnny Walker Red	$24.99/ 1.75 liters	$32.99/ 1.75 liters	$11.69/375 ml.
Smirnoff Vodka	$12.89/ 1.75 liters	$15.99/ 1.75 liters	$9.99/750 ml.
Budweiser	$13.39/30 ($.45/can)	$14.99/24 ($.62/can)	$4.99/6 ($.83/can)
Marlboro Cigarettes	$16.49/ carton ($1.65/pack)	$22.59/ carton ($2.26/pack)	$2.35/pack

On average, for every $100 the Costco shopper spends on booze and smokes, the Safeway buyer will spend $133 and the corner store shopper a whopping $182.

For marijuana, I assumed a daily consumption of one $10 bag (2 to 4 joints) of good-quality commercial. This amounts to about 1,000 joints, or one pound, per year. I then compared the annual cost of buying by the "dime bag" to buying the pound all at once. The retail buyer would pay about $3,650 for the year's usage, while the pound buyer (presumably rich) would pay about $1,000– a 73% saving.

For heroin, I took the estimate of the Office of National Drug Control Policy that a "hardcore" user averages $208/week, then applied the estimated current retail price of heroin of $1.00 per pure milligram to calculate that the "hardcore" user consumes about 10,800 milligrams per year. I then imagined that a rich addict was able to buy a year's supply all at once– i.e., about one-half ounce (14 grams) of 75% pure heroin. Such a buyer, if well-connected, could score his heroin for about $2,000– an 81% saving on the $10,800 that the "retail" buyer would pay.

The same huge savings advantage applies to someone fortunate enough to buy cocaine by the ounce rather than by the "rock" or the gram. Notice, however, that as we move from legal substances toward powerful, illicit ones, the advantages of the rich buyer are more problematic:

- The rich don't always have better access than the poor to wholesale sources.
- Denial, for rich or poor, shortens the time frame: "I'm not really hooked, and will probably not use after tomorrow."
- Anyone's addictive usage can be chaotic; one's entire stash can be consumed in a single "run".

With cigarettes and marijuana, and especially with heroin and cocaine, the rich think and act like the poor: one's purchase and consumption is a matter of coping day-by-day.

The AIDS Treatment Scene: Egalitarianism at Last

If heroin and cocaine make the rich like the poor, AIDS treatment– at least in the exceptional case of San Francisco– can make the poor like the rich. AIDS advocates here have aggressively sought, and largely won, commitments to full access to treatment for all San Franciscans, regardless of ability to pay. To quote from the recommendations of *An*

HIV/AIDS Policy Agenda for San Francisco, published in 1997 by the San Francisco AIDS Foundation:

"San Francisco should maintain its financial commitment to ensure continued access to– and no wait lists for– HIV / AIDS treatments if state and federal funds are threatened."

"The City should continue to fund drugs needed by people with HIV / AIDS that are not covered by the state's ADAP."

"The City should work to stabilize the housing, mental health, and substance abuse problems of people living with HIV / AIDS, and develop systems and programs to help individuals adhere to the drug dosing schedules, particularly for those who are homeless, mentally ill, and / or substance users."

"Health care providers must be required to meet the same goals for quality care, reimbursement mechanisms and consumer information, regardless of funding source."

"The City...should continue to move towards substance abuse treatment on demand, and increase the funding accordingly."

"San Francisco must create additional housing, including the renovation and rehabilitation of existing buildings, and make efficient use of existing housing stock, such as that on Treasure Island and in the Presidio."

Wow. These recommendations add up to nothing short of a commitment to raise impoverished HIV+ people to middle-class status, at least in the context of their struggle with HIV disease. That's the reverse of the cocaine paradox: the poor are helped to deal with life as the rich do. This is an earthshaking idea, often derided by critics as "AIDS exceptionalism" or "a huge public expenditure on one disease at the neglect of other diseases." But the expense is likely to be well worth it: AIDS patients will become taxpaying workers, HIV contagion will be suppressed, injection drug users will be put on the road to recovery, and the morale of the community will be enhanced. The case in favor of a "San Francisco model" of comprehensive AIDS treatment is so strong that one is inspired to regard this model not as "exceptionalism" but as the standard by which all other major diseases should be treated. In brief: provide people a decent level of stability and prosperity and they'll have fewer diseases and, being healthier, they'll be more productive and pay more taxes.

Contrariwise, the HIV treatment arena in San Francisco does not provide the usual advantages to the rich. The best AIDS physicians are not concentrated in the elite private hospitals or healthcare plans, and there are no advantages to buying triple-combination medications in bulk– the retail price of key meds such as Crixivan has already been cut to the wholesale level by Stadtlanders and other enlightened pharmacies.

The advice we AIDS activists give to the man on the street– "use drugs and/or have sex in a safer manner now, and you'll avoid a terrible disease ten years from now" and "get on this AIDS cocktail regimen now and you won't get sick next year"– is keyed to a middle-class time frame, namely the distant future. The irony is that our success may depend on bringing the full range of bourgeois advantages– steady jobs, good housing, healthy lifestyles, stable relationships, superb medical care– to junkies, speed-freaks, party-circuit boys, and the homeless.

AIDS and Class

An enduring truth of human history is that class (a.k.a. socioeconomic status) makes a big difference in the way disease is experienced. As compared to the rich, the poor get sick more, obtain less succor, endure more pain, and die younger. It's not just that the rich have more money; they also are usually (not always) more educated, well-connected, politically powerful, and optimistic. They also have healthier diets, less stress, cleaner environments, less substance abuse, better medical care, and a clearer view of their distant future. All of these factors are conducive to a longer, healthier life. In the face of illness, then, class is far more important than race or even gender (ask yourself: would you rather face a dangerous disease as a rich black woman, or as a poor white man?)

HIV disease is no exception. The advantages of higher class are actually enhanced, in view of access to expensive treatment and the complexity of medication regimens. Ironically, HIV appeared just as the bourgeoisie in America began winning an impressive string of victories in the class war: since 1981, the aggregate net worth of the rich has doubled, while the income of the poor has declined.

So, class is obviously a big factor insofar as it relates to HIV disease. But it's hard to get good data on the matter. Public health authorities in the U.S. keep good statistics on the age, sex, race, and risky behaviors of people with AIDS, but rarely keep data on education, occupation, or income, and never on net worth. Lacking decent data, the best I can do is to offer a taxonomy. Here are five different sorts or "lists" of people with AIDS, depending on how much resources they can marshal in their personal struggle:

A-list PWAs: This class of people with AIDS (PWAs) can self-pay medical care (even the most costly and rarefied sort) if necessary, and can live comfortably for a long time without working.

B-list: These PWAs are middle-class and educated. They have health insurance and know how to work the system. A long costly struggle against AIDS would deplete their savings, but not dispossess them from their homes.

P-list: These are working class people without much net worth or "home equity". In dealing with AIDS, however, they have a well-developed support structure: family, church, neighborhood, co-workers, Union, and suchlike. They may lose their jobs, but usually will have a place to live.

L-list: These are PWAs who are both lower-class and lacking in a support network. They can (just) keep their lives together, until advancing symptoms render them jobless, benefitless, and/or homeless.

X-list: In this category are underclass PWAs who are not only poor, but have a hostile relationship to the larger society because of criminal activity, homelessness, or madness.

This taxonomy offers, I hope, the means to begin an analysis of class and AIDS. My first postulate is that the relative size of the groups in America changes over time. I hazard that the P- and L-lists are gradually increasing at the expense of the A- and B-lists. The main reason for this is that, lately, HIV affects gay men less, and injection drug users and their sexual partners more. I also postulate that the X-list is slowly shrinking, because most of the at-risk people of that sort were long ago hit hard by HIV.

My rough guesses as to the PWA percentages of A's, B's, P's, L's, and X's are these:

	In 1985:	In 1997:
A's	6%	2%
B'S	33%	23%
P's	30%	45%
L's	20%	25%
X's	11%	10%

San Francisco's Exceptionality

San Francisco is a striking exception to the general rule that class predicts HIV disease experience. The reason is that this city has a uniquely well-developed and egalitarian system of care. This system, maintained with great effort and devotion, has largely guaranteed that the P-list, L-list, and even X-list PWAs can enjoy:

- decent housing [HOPWA]

- regular, nutritious meals [Open Hand]

- competent primary care, free at the point of delivery [SF General Hospital, Haight-Ashbury Free Clinics, etc.]

- information on how to get into experimental medications protocols [Project Inform]

- assistance in obtaining a full range of social benefits [AIDS Benefits Counselors]

- transportation assistance [Shanti, etc.]

- services for HIV-related mental impairment [Continuum]

- home care by visiting medical personnel [Visiting Nurses, Shanti, etc.]

and much else besides. The result is that, in San Francisco more than anywhere else in the world, the poor do not experience AIDS in a vividly different way than the rich. If a community is judged "by how well it treats the least among itself," our City will surely be ranked among the great.

Sick and Poor, Sick and Rich

In his book, *Unhealthy Societies: The Afflictions of Inequality,* Richard Wilkinson shows that health is directly related to social class: the nearer you are to the bottom of the social ladder, the sicker you are likely to be and the younger you are likely to die. If you're poor, you leave school earlier, you have children earlier, your organs wear out earlier, and you grow old before your time. Television, smoking, and alcohol are about the only kinds of recreation you can afford. When you're sick, you'll wait a long time to see a doctor who'd probably prefer working elsewhere. Added to these obvious consequences of poverty, Wilkinson argues, are two less tangible factors that augment the disadvantage of the poor: higher stress and lesser social cohesion.[1]

To illustrate these "Afflictions of Inequality", let's contrast "Harry", a rich American from a rich family, with "Bill", a man poor all his life, as each copes with HIV infection. There are many ways in which Harry is better off:

---

1 The role of stress in health was elucidated in a decades-long followup study of 18,000 male British civil servants. It was found that the lowest employment grades had four times the rate of heart attacks as the highest, apparently because "lack of control in one's workplace" results in higher stress. The importance of social cohesion was demonstrated in a study of Italian immigrants and their descendants in Roseto, PA. The first generation, in spite of a diet of rich traditional foods, had heart attacks at half the U.S. rate. Later generations, having "assimilated" into American patterns– and away from tight-knit Italian community traditions– had heart attacks at the usual U.S. rate.

Harry has much more money than Bill.

He can pay his own medical bills if need be. He can also travel far in pursuit of just the right doctor or pharmacy.

Harry can have people do tasks that would otherwise run down his energies. He can hire maids, send out his laundry, and order in his meals.

Harry can buy things that directly impact his health, such as protein-rich foods, filtered water, and vitamins. He can also furnish his life with things that indirectly affect health through stress reduction or morale enhancement, for example a good stereo system, cable TV, flowers, and nice clothes. Harry can also afford to keep in touch with distant friends– or HIV experts– by regular long-distance phone calls.

Bill has no access to credit or even a credit card. Harry's resources are vast, even compared to the $200,000 or more it may cost him to battle HIV disease for a lifetime.

Bill is obliged to spend most of his time near where he lives. Harry, if he wants, can take vacations just about whenever and wherever.

When Bill travels around town, he's much more reliant on public transportation, with all of its attendant stresses and (especially in winter) communicable diseases. Harry can drive his own (well-maintained) car or use cabs.

Harry lives in a nicer neighborhood.

His home is quiet and "healing". He has more living space, which is cleaner because he hires people to keep it so. If he must maintain a complex 30-pill-per-day HIV medications regimen, his living space– clocks, refrigerators, privacy, etc.– will be conducive.

Bill lives in a more dangerous neighborhood, which inhibits even such daily routines as taking a walk or going to the neighborhood store. And at the store, the reception is wary and the prices high. Some of the neighbors have a notorious tendency to prey upon the weak. All this adds to stress.

Bill's home is much more likely to be invaded by burglars, or by cops impatiently pursuing drug dealers.

The hospitals and clinics in Harry's neighborhood are better. The wait for care is shorter, the waiting rooms are pleasanter, and the staff treat the patients more respectfully.

Harry has had more education, at better schools.

He can read and understand the labels and other literature pertinent to his HIV medications.

Thanks to his superior education, Harry is better able to beguile the tedium of long bedridden days by reading, listening to music, conversing with friends, or just thinking. Bill is much more dependent on television.

Harry is far likelier than Bill to own a computer with Internet access, and to know how to use it to search worldwide for HIV-related treatment information.

Bill is susceptible to "miracle cures", and also to paranoid ideas along the lines of, "AIDS is a CIA plot against the poor." Harry has a healthy skepticism about such things.

Harry is much more aware of the history of human diseases and of his role in that history.

<u>Harry's friends are mostly rich and well-educated, like him, while Bill's friends are mostly poor and badly-educated, like him.</u>

Harry has a lot of people from whom he can borrow money if need be.

Harry is also able to borrow quiet spaces for healing, for example a friend's home in the country.

Harry can learn about HIV meds, and even be given them, by friends who are knowledgeable about HIV. Harry may even have several friends who are themselves physicians.

Bill's friends are far more likely to have irrational or paranoid ideas about HIV, healthcare, doctors, and suchlike. The stories he hears from them only exacerbate his anxiety and hopelessness.

<u>Nowadays, bourgeois culture is healthier than proletarian culture.</u>

Bill's diet consists of too much fatty foods, and too few green vegetables and fruits. Even if Bill wanted fresh fruits and vegetables, the stores near his home don't stock them.

Bill gets much less exercise than Harry.

Harry relates to his family and friends in a more healthful, functional way, possibly because they have hired psychiatrists, counselors, family therapists, etc., to work through problems.

Harry's belief in his own personal efficacy is far greater than Bill's.

Bourgeois culture plans for the future. Thus Harry is far better able than Bill to envision the world ten years hence, and to see himself in it.

Bill has had more brutalizing experiences– fights, crimes, family abuse, hunger, unemployment, classism, perhaps racism. The social cohesion of his neighborhood steadily deteriorates, while Harry's world is, if anything, becoming more cohesive.

If Bill's HIV disease is compounded by addiction to an illicit substance, he must face the additional problems of dangerous trafficking, contaminated drugs, police hassles, and perhaps imprisonment. If Harry is addicted, he's likelier to have a "cleaner" connection for his drugs, and his bourgeois status assures kinder treatment by cops and judges.

What Is To Be Done?

From this long and melancholy listing, it is obvious that a poor person fighting HIV disease is hugely disadvantaged, in terms of stress and social cohesion as well as the more obvious factors of wealth, education, and living environment. Moreover, the proportion of "Bills" among Americans living with HIV is now more than one in three, while the proportion of "Harrys" has dropped since 1985 from about 6% to about 2% (see "AIDS and Class", p. 106.)

What is to be done? First off, we should reexamine the data to see if what is true for other diseases is also true for HIV. Our hypothesis would be:

> HIV-infected people of high socioeconomic status (SES) have more favorable outcomes of their HIV disease than those of low SES, other factors being equal.

I predict that the data will show that the poor are much worse off than the rich. If so, the most obvious remedy would be a social revolution resulting in redistribution of wealth and genuine equality of opportunity. But this is not in the cards; I expect to grow old and simple, like Mother Jones, in fruitless waiting for that glorious day. Nonetheless, there are important ways in which we can intervene to help the poor face HIV as if they were rich. Another essay ("AIDS and Class") describes how a superb "system of care" has largely achieved this in San Francisco, mostly by allocating resources– nutritious meals, competent primary care, good information, mental-health services, home care, etc.– directly to the needy. Perhaps our City's system of care would be even better if we also set lower stress and better social cohesion as service goals. To that end, I offer these hypotheses:

> HIV+ people who consistently attend Twelve Step groups will have more favorable outcomes of HIV disease than those not in such groups, other factors (SES, etc.) being equal.
>
> HIV+ people who live in intentional communities (e.g., Delancey Street) or in extended families will have more favorable outcomes than those who live alone, other factors being equal.

HIV+ people who are involved in communities of faith, such as Glide Memorial Church, will have more favorable outcomes than those not thus involved, other factors being equal.

HIV+ first-generation Latino immigrants will have more favorable outcomes than second- or third-generation Latino-Americans, other factors being equal.

HIV+ people who consistently deal with stress by medication (such as Prozac) or other methods (such as meditation) will have more favorable outcomes than those who don't deal with their stress, other factors being equal.

HIV+ people who live in rural areas will have more favorable outcomes than those who live in the inner city, other factors (especially isolation and loneliness) being equal.

If research supports some or all of these hypotheses, it will show the way toward further improvements in San Francisco's system of care- and help the thousands of HIV+ Bills in our City to cope more successfully with their infection.

IV.

THE GAY WORLD

The gay world consists not merely of the A-list and the B-list, but of seven more "letters", as explained in "Alphabet of Gaydom". "Telephone Strategies" asks you whether you're One Who Calls or One Who Is Called, and suggests that your love life will suffer from the wrong combinations. "Finishing Golden Boys" proposes a school for young male geishas, to the benefit of all. "Cock Size" is a statistical examination of how the claims of 'escorts' jibe with reality. "Short and Tall Men Together" imagines a club catering to the intense attraction that short and tall men often have for one another. Seven innovative ways to help youths avoid HIV are set forth in "Prevention for Gay Men". It's sometimes hard to get gay men to practice safe sex; "A Modest Proposal" suggests hiring beautiful rent boys to show them how it's done. "Stories from the Closet" is an account of my own pre-Stonewall college days.

A Two-Dimensional Diagram of Male Fashion

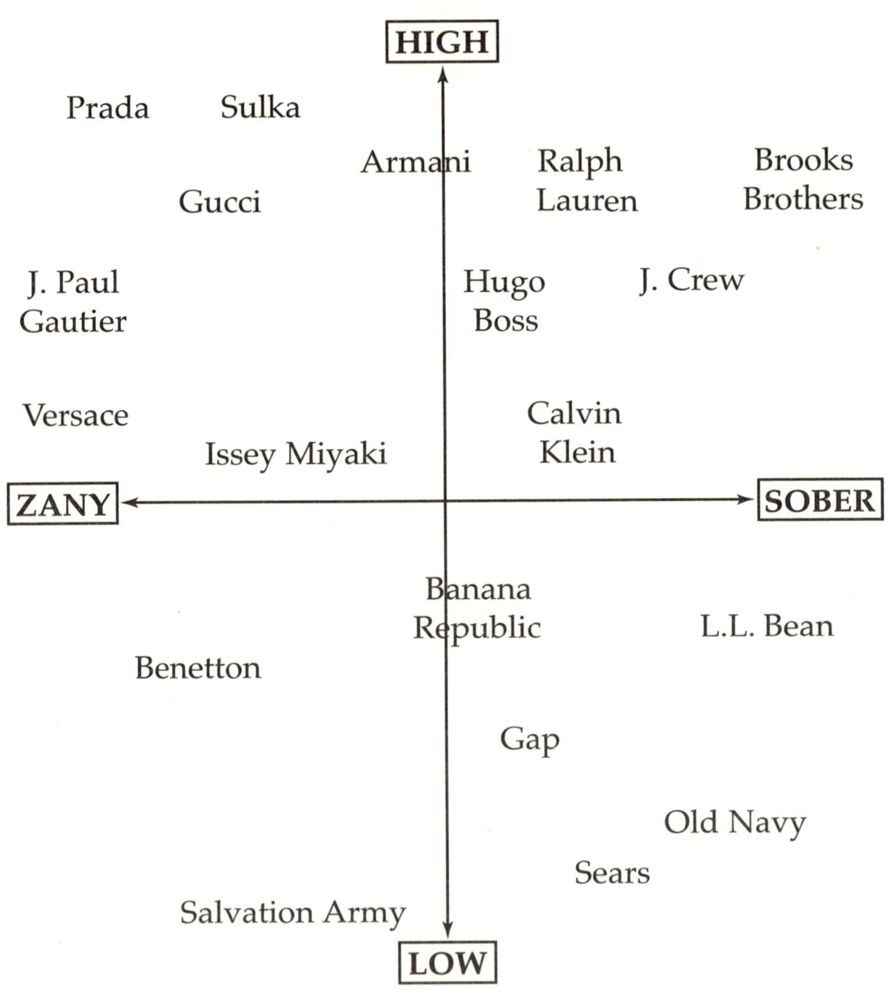

The Alphabet of Gaydom

In *Tales of the City,* Armistead Maupin introduced us to the "A-gays" and "B-gays", his adaptation of the "A-list" and "B-list" to the gay scene. As a social psychologist, I was uncomfortable with the notion that all of gaydom could be assigned to just two classes. I resolved to make a thorough study of the matter.

My diligent research revealed that there are no fewer than <u>nine</u> social categories of gay men, with A-gays and B-gays together amounting to no more than 15% of the "alphabet". Allow me to elucidate, beginning with Armistead's alpha and beta.

(1) **A-gays** (Attitude, Grade A) are the aspiring aristocrats of the system. For them, it's nothing but the best– the best clothes, the best parties, the most prestigious company. *GQ, Vanity Fair,* and *Architectural Digest* are the magazines of choice. Quite often their pretensions outdo their achievements, but their wit is sharp and their social graces well-honed. The A-gays almost always look good, and are willing to devote much time and artifice to that end. But A's are easily bored and are apt to be sour and irritated if they feel they're among the wrong crowd. Only about one in fifty gays is an A, but this proportion can be as high as one in ten in some districts of Los Angeles, New York, or Paris. Truman Capote in the 1950s and 1960s was a quintessential A-gay.

(2) **B-gays** (Bourgeois, Grade B) are a lot like A-gays. One can invite them to fill out an A-gay party, and they will behave themselves quite nicely. There are four or five B's to every A, which is suitable because the former act as dough to the latter's yeast. The B-gays are on average just as accom-

plished in their careers as the A-gays, and many of them are socially ambitious and savor the company of the A's. But they lack that certain quality of grace, of "flash", of confident ease– somehow riotous laughter doesn't emanate from their groups as it does from knots of A's. The B's are the pillars of the gay community, intelligent men with important jobs who can be relied upon to attend fund-raisers and support causes. Though only a minority of B-gays are Republican, most gay Republicans are B's.

(3) **R-gays** are the Regular guys of the community. Like Michael Tolliver in *Tales of the City,* they take the role of Everyman in the great morality play of gay life. The R's are the most numerous of the gay alphabet, comprising perhaps one-third of the total– and in small towns, as much as one-half. They are the fellows you see washing their Hondas on a Saturday morning, or shopping by twos at the supermarket, or convening all-male Thanksgiving dinners with sweet enthusiasm. There's nothing particularly impressive about their careers, or their family backgrounds, or their bank balances. They lack pretension and social ambition, but they are very keen about their lovers and the worthy enterprise of making a home and a life together.

(4) The **T-gays** or "Twinkies" are prominent players in the gay life, conspicuous in the full gamut of vealcake media from Calvin Klein ads to X-rated films. They are well-endowed with youth and beauty, if not character. Most of them are quite sweet-tempered, but perhaps also shy and confused. As time passes, however, their move (promotion?) to another category is inevitable. Age 25 is the limit of T-dom for most men, but short guys can go on and on provided they remain sweet *and slender*. Truman Capote was a T-gay in the 1940s, briefly.

(5) **Q-gays** (Queens) can't hide it. They are the only gay type that you can immediately recognize over the telephone. In 2000 as in 1900, they're the ones who are in touch with the Woman within. And in 2000 as in 1900, the Q-gay is the image of "gay" for much of the straight world– and the butt of straight derision and prejudice. Whether we admit it or not, all of gaydom are indebted to the Q-gays who bear the brunt of it. Moreover, they add a great amount of sheer *fun* to the world.

(6) **P-gays** (Punk, Political) are cultural, if not political, rebels. They can usually be recognized by their style: black colors, oversized clothing, strange hair, piercing in quite unexpected body parts. This expresses a conformity to the non-conformity of rebellion against gay (or other) "good taste", but P-gays are capable of much original thought outside matters of culture. They are smarter than they look.

(7) **S-gays** are the Shy fellows of the gay world. Their dress and speech are inconspicuous and ordinary, or even nerdy. An S-gay may be rich with talent or wisdom, but simply disinclined to show it. But in the private audience of a special friend or lover, an amazing display of brilliance, or passion, or color can be coaxed forth...

(8) **X-gays** (as in X-rated) are the hard-core users of gay culture. They're the ones in the bars, or the sex clubs, in the *daytime*. They incline to leather, tobacco, and tattoos. X-gays may lack wit, but their sense of humor– a combination of generous goodfellowship, wide experience, and an utter lack of pretension– is second to none. They have thick skins and remarkable powers of endurance.

(9) **E-gays** (Exceptional, Eccentric) are queer among queers. They have looked at gay life, chosen the forms that suit them

best, and added some zany bits of their own. E-gays are the real originators of much of gay culture– bits of the high style of the A's, the glorious drag of the Q's, the revolutionary politics of the P's– but their imaginations are too fertile and restless to construct an identity around any of it. From early boyhood, they had little or no guilt or shame about their sexuality– and in adulthood, they take great pleasure from homoeroticism, yet being "gay" is only a small part of their sense of self. The best gay writers (Gore Vidal, Oscar Wilde) are usually E's.

On any sunny Saturday afternoon in San Francisco's Castro district, one can observe specimens of each of these gay letters walking about. It is pure pleasure to savor this glorious diversity of gay manhood, and it amazes me that some sour souls walk among this richness, see only the half-dozen or so panhandlers, and complain about how the Castro has "gone to seed"!

I claim that this diversity of gaydom has prevailed for at least seventy years. I am sure that in Cocteau's Paris of the Twenties, one would have seen every one of the nine types, although the R-gay would have been much rarer, and the P-gay much different in appearance, than nowadays.

Having spelled out this alphabet of gaydom, I now must concede that it is on a fast track to obsolescence. Gay men mix together, and celebrate diversity, as never before. Just as the mixing of races in California is slowly blurring away "pure" ethnic identities, mixing within the gay world combines and blends the types. We can look forward to endless combinations– of A/X gays (Truman Capote in the 1980s), or P/Q men, or R/P/S gays– as we adopt and adapt creatively from the rich alphabet soup that the past generation of gay culture has offered up. And as with the races, the proportion of gay cross-breeds increases without limit at the expense of the purebreds.

Why nine "letters" in the Alphabet of Gaydom, and not more or fewer? My theory is that they are the outcome of three "directions of self-development" to which gay men devote their lives:

- **Getting Experience** in the gay social and sexual worlds.
- **Rising in the World** to a higher class.
- **Becoming More Creative** or imaginative, or original, or radical.

I hypothesize that all gay men at age 15 are T-gays. T-dom is an *ur*-state, an origin from which one evolves to other states depending upon the forms of self-development one successfully accomplishes. The combinations of successful development account for seven more letters of the alphabet:

	Getting Experience	**Rising in the World**	**Becoming More Creative**
X	+		
B		+	
P			+
A	+	+	
Q	+		+
S		+	+
E	+	+	+

The greatest number of gay men try to accomplish all three of the forms of development, but are only partially successful in each. Hence the ninth or middling letter: the R-gays.

Telephone Strategies as an Impediment to Homoerotic Love

Every day there are thousands of occasions where two fellows conceive an attraction for one another and exchange phone numbers, with the intention of "call me and let's get together!" However, a large portion of these intentions fail to bear fruit, *even when both men keenly desire it*. The main reason is the mismatch of "telephone strategies".

There are essentially five different Telephone Strategies, divided into the two broad categories of the "ones who call" and the "ones who are called". To use an athletic metaphor, the former play "forward" and the latter "defense". Most (but not all) tops are the Ones Who Call, and most (but not all) bottoms are the Ones Who Are Called.

Here are the five Telephone Strategies, ordered from the most "forward" to the most "defensive".

Ones Who Call

A Will call and will leave message

B Will call, but won't leave message; insist on speaking to the real person

Ones Who Are Called

C Will answer and will return calls

D Monitor calls for desirability and will return calls from a desirable caller

E Monitor calls for desirability but will not return calls

The problem arises from the interaction of these types. Unless one of the men is willing, at least temporarily, to play the role of the One Who Calls, the pair will *never get in touch*. When both are Ones Who Call, contact will be swift, although perhaps less so if both prefer Strategy B. Here are all the possible matches between the five Telephone Strategies, with an estimate of how soon the pair will be able to set a time and place for that crucial First Date:

	A	**B**	**C**	**D**	**E**
A	very soon	soon	very soon	soon	eventually
B	soon	eventually	eventually	never	never
C	very soon	eventually	never	never	never
D	soon	never	never	never	never
E	eventually	never	never	never	never

The most intriguing are the combinations B/D and B/E: although B is willing to call, even repeatedly, contact is *never* made because B hangs up instead of starting to leave a message so that the "monitoring" D or E can pick up the phone.

This analysis reveals a huge impediment to getting together: there will never be a First Date for 13 of the 25 Strategy combinations, and there will be serious delays for another 5 combinations. If gay men are distributed evenly among the Strategies, there will be no connection in 52% of the cases where a pair of men desire it.

Obviously, the solution is to print the above table as a wallet-size card for wide distribution among gay men. Then, when they exchange numbers, a pair of men can check their match of Telephone Strategies. If they find their match is unpropitious, they should set a time and place for the First Date right then, rather than risk never seeing one another again.

The Telephone Strategies problem is alleviated if the One Who Is Called owns a high-tech phone with Caller ID service. Then "monitoring" is effective in all the A/D, A/E, B/D, and B/E combinations, so long as the One Who Is Called can recognize the phone number of the desirable caller.

In the near future gay men may start exchanging E-mail addresses rather than phone numbers. Here the world of gay men divides into the Ones Who Send Mail and the Ones Who Respond. There is no monitoring– except for options such as "Buddies Online"– and one has no choice but to leave messages; therefore, the above categories collapse into A's and D's. The only problem for a mutually admiring pair of men, then, is to make sure that at least one prefers the One Who Sends Mail strategy.

Finishing Golden Boys

or, The Making of a Male Geisha

An occasional coupling in our society is that between a good-looking young man and an older, richer man. We'll call them, respectively, the "Golden Boy" and the "Gentleman". The Gentleman sets the agenda and pays the bills, while the Golden Boy provides attractive companionship and other pleasant services.

The only problem I see here is that power in this relationship is so heavily weighted toward the Gentleman. Not only is he richer and better-connected, he has an enormous advantage in knowledge, experience, and what the French call "savoir-faire". I propose that we redress this imbalance by giving lots of Golden Boys a "finishing school" education. This education will enable Golden Boys to bring as much, or more, savoir-faire to a relationship as their Gentlemen friends. No longer will the younger man be crude and awkward. His tastes will be broadened– for example, if he chooses to play Madonna rather than Mozart on the CD, he will be able to articulate just *why* Madonna is the more felicitous choice for the occasion.

I propose that the first finishing school be established near Boston, a New England city with a long tradition of excellence in higher education. The school will be called the *Augustan Academy,* in honor of a promising 18-year-old youth named Octavian who was "adopted" by Julius Caesar. Octavian– later known as Augustus Caesar– is an ideal exemplar of a Golden Boy, in that he showed that loyal service to a patron can result in a fulfilling life and a nice inheritance.

The Augustan Academy will admit boys between 15 and 19 who show promise for careers as Golden Boys because they (1) are gay or bisexual, (2) enjoy the company of older men, and (3) are inclined more to the domestic arts than to business or the professions. The Academy would provide these boys with two- or three-year courses of study, covering these subjects:

Conversational French
Conversational Italian
Elegant spoken and written English
Music appreciation
Art/design/architecture appreciation
Introduction to world geography and culture
Investment management
Household management
Gourmet cooking
Hosting of dinner parties and cocktail parties

There would, of course, be significant opportunities for physical education and sports, principally:

Aerobics	Skiing
Bodybuilding	Horsemanship
Gymnastics	Sailing
Swimming	Ballroom Dancing

In the last two weeks of the students' final Spring semester, they would be treated to a "Graduation Cruise" to the Bahamas. This cruise would feature a variety of informal and formal meals, cocktail receptions, dances, and other events at which newly-developed social skills could be manifested

The Augustan Academy would be funded partly through tuition paid by the students' families, but mostly by scholarships provided by interested Gentlemen. These scholarships would enable especially promising, but indigent, students to complete their studies. In return for their generosity, the Gentlemen donors would be invited to join in the Graduation Cruise.

Gentlemen, too, will gain from their involvement with the Augustan Academy. They will be reminded that learning is a lifelong process; that original thought often emerges from quite young minds; that great art and music is created by each new generation; that keeping oneself healthy and fit is much appreciated by boyfriends; and that love between generations can be enduring and profoundly enriching.

Cock Size in Gay Escorts Ads

Most newspapers that are oriented to the gay male community, such as the *Bay Area Reporter* in San Francisco or *Edge* in Los Angeles, contain a number of advertisements for "escorts" and "models". It is not hard to deduce that nearly all of the advertisers in those categories are offering sexual services. One peculiar characteristic of these ads is that many of them contain some reference to the large penis size of the "escort". Adjectives such as "endowed", "hung", or "big" are especially common. It occurred to me that a statistical analysis could be fruitful.

I started with three basic assumptions:

(1) **The population of "escorts" is generally not different from other American males in terms of cock size.** The length of the erect cocks of young American men has been extensively analyzed by the Kinsey Institute of Sex Research. These lengths are distributed in a normal or "bell" curve with a mean length of 6.1 inches and a standard deviation of .6 inch— that is, 68% of cocks will measure between 5.5 and 6.7 inches, 95% between 4.9 and 7.3 inches, and so forth.

(2) **There is, however, a modest "Jeff Stryker effect":** a handful of individuals are motivated to begin careers as "escorts" because of extraordinary penile endowment.

(3) **There is a systematic tendency to overestimate deviations above the mean.** This has been widely observed in people's misestimation of the height of very tall people— a 6'6" man is thought to be "seven feet tall", or a 7'1" basketball player is said to be "eight feet tall". The misestimation seems to average about 7 units for every 4 units of real dif-

ference from the mean. Thus, when one sees a cock four-tenths of an inch longer than average, he or she will reckon that it is actually seven-tenths of an inch longer. There is a simple reason for this misestimation: volume is proportional to the cube of length, so that a 7.5″ cock has about twice the volume of a 6.0″ cock if the two are shaped the same. Also, as was pointed out to F. Scott Fitzgerald, if two fellows are sized exactly the same each will think the other is bigger. It has to do with the angle of the view...

I examined the full complement of "escorts" ads from the January 4, 1990 issue of the *Bay Area Reporter* and from the December 6, 1989 issue of *Edge*. There were 80 such ads in the *B.A.R.* and 31 in the *Edge*. I counted any references to cock size, then converted these references to "perceived length" in inches as they might be (mis)estimated by a typical observer. Results were as follows:

Perceived Length	Description in Ad	N
***B. A. R.* Group (N=80)**		
5″	"Small endowment"	1
6″	[no reference to size]	42
	"Thick" or "Extra thick"	2
7″	"Big", "Hung", Hung big", "Well hung", or "7 inches"	16
7 1/2″	"Extra hung"	6
8″	"Horse hung"	1
	"Super endowed"	1
	"8 inches"	3
8 1/2″	"Enormous long"	1
9″	"9 inches"	3
9 1/2″	"9 1/2 inches"	1
10″	"10 inches"	2
10 1/2″	"10 1/2 inches"	1

Edge Group (N=31)		
6″	[no reference to size]	20
7″	"Endowed"	9
7 1/2″	"Big endowment"	1
8″	"Endowed huge"	1

I have made the assumption that these "perceived length" categories correspond to "true length" ranges, according to the 7/4 exaggeration ratio described above. The following table summarizes the findings (there is some overlap between the length categories):

Perceived Length	True Length	*B.A.R.* numbers	*Edge* numbers	Percent of young men in range
6″ or less	up to 6.5″	45 (56%)	20 (65%)	75%
7″	6.5″ to 6.9″	16 (20%)	9 (29%)	16%
7 1/2″	6.9″ to 7.2″	6 (7%)	1 (3%)	6%
8″	7.1″ to 7.5″	5 (6%)	1 (3%)	4%
8 1/2″	7.4″ to 7.6″	1 (1%)	0	.9%
9″	7.5″ to 8.1″	3 (4%)	0	.9%
9 1/2″ to 10 1/2″	8.1″ to 8.7″	4 (5%)	0	.05%

The estimated "true" lengths for the cocks of the *B.A.R.* men seem to have a fairly good "fit" with the distribution for young American men in general. Fully 44% make some claim as to being "hung", "big", etc., so it would appear that fellows as short as 6.5″ or even 6.4″ or 6.3″ are making the most of a slight deviation above the mean. The seven who actually claim to have nine inches or more are a bit of a puzzle. Even after correcting for the phenomenon of innocent exaggeration, these fellows would all measure at least 7.5 inches— a condition of fewer than one young American man in 100. Since their claims are subject to verification by (possibly numerous) respondents to their ads, I can only conclude that their claims have stood up to review. Aside from these seven, the "escorts" of San Francisco seem not different from the ordinary run of young American men.

The Los Angeles men advertising in *Edge* appear also to "fit" very well with the distribution of young men as a whole. However, there is no discernible "Jeff Stryker effect"— no one claimed nine inches or more. Also, it is curious that every one of the eleven Angelenos who claimed bigness used the word "endowment" or "endowed", while only 1 out of 35 San Franciscans did. This may reflect regional peculiarities of Northern v. Southern California sexual vernacular.

All of the above analysis depends on the accuracy of my translation of phallic self-description into "perceived" and then into "true" inches. And of course many of the advertisers might not have measured themselves in the conventional way (along the top) done by Kinsey's sample. But I still make this claim: in spite of their understandable tendency to exaggerate as much as they can get away with, the cock size of "escorts" distributes in the same bell curve as for young men in general, with a noticeable bulge at the right-hand end due to the "Jeff Stryker effect" of specialized recruitment.

One final point: why is there such keen interest in big cocks? Are we to assume that bigger is better? Bigness may be the majority preference, but it is not unanimous; I am certain that some gay men prefer a small endowment in their sexual partners. In the ads sampled from the two newspapers, 48 men claimed that they were notably big; but one boldly advertised himself as having "small endowment". It would be interesting to know if that one "small" man got more responses than the average of the 48 "large" men. I'd be willing to bet that he did.

Short and Tall Men Together

It was one of those clean sunny San Francisco afternoons early in May. My friend Mark and I were having cappuccinos at the Cafe Flore. He was telling me about a new organization for gay men, "Short and Tall Men Together". Incredulous that such a thing could exist, I had all sorts of questions.

"What you're not seeing is that the difference is itself a turn-on," declared Mark. "The contrast is something the short guy and the tall guy find endlessly fascinating— it's like the race difference is a turn-on for black-white couples, or the sex difference for hetero couples."

"Well, I can see what people like in tall fellows," I replied, stealing a glance at his 6'3" frame and yard-wide shoulders. "But what is it about short guys? Seems to me nobody has ever said, 'too little of a good thing'!"

"Hey, come on, Michael— surely you'd agree that a BMW is a more attractive car than a big old Buick?"

"Of course..."

"See, a Beemer is nimble and compact and moves all of a piece, not like a big American car that lumbers this way and that on the road. Short men have that Beemer quality— they're much more likely to be nimble and acrobatic."

"But most athletes are big guys...", I protested.

"Sure— they're big because they have to crash through a football line, or jump up to a basketball hoop, or do some other beefy task. But they're not much fun to watch— they just don't have grace. They're so long that when they move, their top part is going one way while the bottom part is going the other, like a car pulling a trailer on a bumpy road!"

"*You* don't look like that," I exclaimed, "I think you look just great when you move!"

"Well, I feel awkward when I compare myself," Mark insisted. "All of the best dancers, acrobats, ice skaters— anything where exquisite precision of movement is needed— are little guys. And some of them are so *foxy*! Frankly, I don't know what they find attractive in a big lout like me, but then, that's the miraculous thing about our 'Short and Tall Men Together' club."

"Now I've heard everything...you mean to tell me that lots of other guys have the same bizarre interests as you?"

"You oughta come see for yourself. The first Thursday night of each month there's at least 200 guys— and we've been doing this for more than a year. We've been renting the Slovenian Hall over on Potrero Hill. We fix up a wooden bar across the front door, at just the right height. To get in, you either have to be able to walk under the bar without stooping, or look over it without stretching. This means that you have to be shorter than five seven or taller than six one to be part of the club..."

"That's a novel approach," I said.

"Yes," Mark replied, "but you see, the key to the whole evening is the pre-party meetings. The dancing doesn't start until ten. Before then, all the tall guys are supposed to go to the downstairs lounge, and all the short ones to the library on the second floor."

"That must be frustrating— sitting around with a bunch of big dudes you're not attracted to."

"Oh, but it's not at all— see, we're all anticipating the dancing to come, so we spend the whole time B.S.ing about short men and how *fine* they are. Like, we talk about whether the ideal height for a man is five five, or five six, or five four. And each week we put up pictures of some superstars— Timothy Goebel, Michael J. Fox. And usually someone has a fabulous story to tell. Last week, this guy Bill told us about spending an afternoon with Bart Conner at Padre Island. We heard every glorious detail! Right down to the way his tan line curved around his tight little...*oooeee*! So, you can imagine, all of us are pretty much worked up into a frenzy of desire by the time 10 o'clock rolls around."

"I suppose the same things happens upstairs with the short guys..."

"Well, of course I haven't actually been up there," he answered, gazing at the back of a little bleached-blond youth at the check stand. "But I do know that they have a collection of photos of Cowboys and 49ers, for that Calvin Klein underwear series–including several shots that they.....umm... couldn't use. So the little guys work themselves into a frenzy, too— and believe me, once we get together on the dance floor, hardly anyone doesn't get asked to dance— we call it the 'ten o'clock stampede'!"

"That must be quite a sight," I said, chuckling at the thought of all the asymmetrical couples. "And I suppose there's a certain amount of going home together..."

"You can be sure of that!" declared Mark, his eyes twinkling at the thought.

"But once you get home, isn't there sometimes a bit of...er...*disappointment*? I mean, short guys aren't likely to be too well endowed..."

"Hmph!" Mark replied testily. "That's the same old stupid prejudice. You can never tell about a guy— you'd be amazed at what you sometimes find inside a pair of 28-inch-waist 501's. And anyway, who's to say that small isn't better? What I said about the whole man goes for his cock too... a small one is more apt to be nicely proportioned. Really, Michael, you gotta get with the flow– small is beautiful, small is better!"

"For you, maybe– but I'm turned on by the easygoing self-confidence of really big men. And I love the feel of a big hunk who's takin' charge!"

"Well, a lot of us big guys like to be taken charge *of*, sometimes!" he exclaimed, as we got up to leave. "Mmm— if you think of a jockey on a horse, you might get the picture..."

"*Now* you've got me interested," I declared. "I sorta wish I could go with you tonight."

"Well, maybe we'll form a group, 'Almost-short and Almost-tall Men Together'", Mark laughed, "then you five-eight guys could take part, if you like!"

"Five seven-and-a-half," I corrected, beaming up at him. "And with a definite idea of what I like!"

"Hey— thanks for the nice thought," replied Mark, grinning,

"You make me feel like the days of us giants aren't coming to an end after all. But you know, I suspect old Mother Earth really appreciates it when people live lightly on her. She likes people that eat fewer pounds of food and wear fewer square yards of clothes. So small isn't just beautiful, it's ecological!"

* * * * * *

I kept thinking about that horse-and-jockey image that evening, as I set about my task: first finding the old pair of loafers, then prying off the heels, then pulling out the nails and sanding smooth the leather. I reflected that tonight was the second time this year that I'd hoped to "pass the bar". I resisted a wild impulse to go shopping for a set of jockey's silks...

Prevention for Gay Men

It is time to get serious about keeping young gay men free from HIV infection. A study published recently by the San Francisco Department of Public Health found a 9.4% HIV+ rate among homosexually active Bay Area men aged 17 to 22. This implies an average annual seroconversion rate of about 2%, which is *simply unacceptable* in an era where older gay men and even injection drug users have achieved annual seroconversion rates on the order of .5% or less.

The seven prevention elements listed below are by no means a comprehensive list, but they constitute a very strong start in that direction. None of them require much money; what is required, rather, is initiative and determination on the part of the prevention community.

(1) Abundant Condoms. Condoms are the single most effective means of protection during insertive sexual intercourse. To the maximum extent possible, they should be around when and where young gay men are about to have sex. Careful thought should be given to the venues where young men are active: not just bars and sex clubs, but dance clubs, parks, street sites, college dorms, and so forth. Of course, condoms should be free or very cheap, and available without delay or embarrassment.

(2) User-Friendly Condoms. The best condoms are those whose package can be opened with one hand, in the dark, in a few seconds. Ideally, the user should not risk being wrong about "which side" of the condom to put on, and also should not be bothered with "squeezing the air out"; this means that pre-lubed, folded condoms are preferable to rolled, unlubed ones. The odor and taste of condoms should be pleasant. Lastly, condom availability should recognize the fact that young men's erections vary greatly in size: of course "one size fits all", but that size can be comfortable for a little fellow but too tight at first for a big fellow. Three sizes ("regular", "large", and "extra large") should suffice.

(3) Condoms for the Receptive Partner. The FDA has approved for sale the "female condom", produced by the Pharmacal Company. A study presented at the VIIth International Conference on AIDS reported universal approval from 20 male couples who used this condom during anal intercourse. To make these "receptive partners' condoms" widely available will empower many more young "bottoms" to protect themselves.

(4) The Lysistrata Club. All pairs of gay men intending to engage in penetrative sex should negotiate and resolve issues of safer sex practices. Ideally, gay male "tops" should be aware that they are simply not acceptable as sex partners unless they carry condoms and use them on all necessary occasions. The word to "tops" should be, "Don't wait to be asked— make it obvious that you wouldn't think of doing it without a condom." One powerful way to encourage such awareness is by enrolling 100 of the handsomest gay men in the Bay Area (all aged under 26 and all "bottoms" at least some of the time) in a "Lysistrata Club". Men in this Club would vow to have no sex with men who won't use condoms consistently. The Club men would proclaim their vow publicly and would wear special enamel "100%" buttons. After each six-month period throughout which this vow was kept, each Club member would receive $500 in cash.

(5) Lubricants. After condoms, the next most effective HIV prevention method is the abundant use of virucidal lubricants. Such lubricants are directly protective for the insertive partner, but they also (even without the virucide) greatly reduce the potential for abrasion and tearing in "rough" or prolonged sex. As with condoms, these should be widely and freely available to gay youths. The lube should be packaged in pocket size containers which can be opened by one hand in the dark. The material should be water-based; the odor and taste should be pleasant; and the potential for staining or difficult cleanup should be minimal.

(6) An Erotophilic Environment. HIV education brochures, pamphlets, and posters have had wide distribution among young Americans. The problem with most of these is that they are wordy and boring. Gay youth would benefit from sex-positive, visually rich, erotically exciting materials specifically designed for them. Models and production values should be in the "Marky Mark" ballpark— that is, "hot" enough to be objects of feverish collection for young gay men. The "message"— on the importance and methodology of safer sex— is easy enough to integrate into these visual images. The potential objections of the straight public should simply be ignored: "It is easier to obtain forgiveness than permission."

(7) Abundant Testing. One more effective measure against contagion is to make as large a percentage as possible of HIV-positive youth aware of their status. HIV antibody testing should be even more widely and readily available than at present, and all those testing positive should have immediate access to generous, comprehensive, and sustained supportive counseling. This should include cash rewards for enrolling in programs which provide early HIV treatment and which enhance and maintain safer sexual practices.

A Modest Proposal

Back in 2001 the Consensus Group estimated that three-quarters of that year's HIV seroconversions in San Francisco would result from homosexual activities among non-injection drug using men. This amounts to about 748 men– a small number compared to that for 1982, to be sure, but nonetheless an avoidably terrible impact among one of the best-served gay communities of the world.

Obviously this male-to-male contagion has been a major target for the City's well-funded prevention effort. There are many factors in the persistence of unsafe sexual practices, but at the core is the failure to negotiate condom use when two men engage in anal sex. I contend that a tiny minority– maybe 3,000 of the City's 47,000 homosexually active men– account for most of these unsafe practices. I would now like to make a modest proposal for an intervention that, I believe, would greatly enhance condom use in that high-risk minority.

High-risk men would be identified at likely places such as sex clubs, late-night dance clubs, drug treatment agencies, and STD treatment facilities. They would be recruited into certain modalities of prevention education, such as individual risk reduction counseling (IRRC) or prevention case management, that have proven efficacious. For simplicity, let's assume that IRRC is the chosen prevention modality. After completing IRRC, each client would be shown a "Sex Worker Portfolio" containing photographs of *very* attractive male "escorts". The client would choose one of these, and a "Direct Experience of Safer Sex" (DESS) session would be scheduled.

The DESS session would consist of sexual intercourse between the client and the Sex Worker, in a venue of the client's choice. The task of the Sex Worker would be to arouse and satisfy the client as much as possible, with accompanying instruction and demonstration of condom usage. This is the main thrust of my "modest proposal": an unforgettable sexual experience intertwined with valuable learning, particularly concerning

- the right time to introduce a condom into sex play;
- effective, sex-positive ways to talk about condoms, especially at first ("Hey, stud, put on this and let's *really* get it on!");
- nonverbal gestures toward the same end.

Some of the clients will be exclusive "bottoms" or exclusive "tops", for whom one DESS session will suffice. The majority, however, will be "versatiles" for whom separate instruction will be needed for both the inserter and receptor roles. For some of these "versatiles", the complete instruction will require a second DESS session, possibly with a different Sex Worker. At the end of the DESS, the client would receive a gift package of condoms and lubricants suited to his (perhaps newly-refined) taste.

Before these DESS trainings can begin, about 30 "instructors" will need to be recruited from among the upper echelons of the City's sex workers. Each would be given four hours of intensive training (for which they would be paid) so that they themselves become able to instruct and demonstrate condom sense. After the training, homoerotic 8x10 photographs of each Sex Worker would be secured for the Portfolio.

Cost Factors

Here is an annual budget for Direct Experience of Safer Sex for 500 clients. The main expense is for upper-echelon sex workers. Male Sex Workers of that quality earn between $100 and $500 per session; I believe we can get by with a standard rate of $200. I estimate that 100 of the "versatile" clients would need to have a second session, with the same or a different Sex Worker, to learn and rehearse safer practices as both "top" and "bottom".

Sex Workers, 600 sessions @ $200	$120,000
Training session payments to 30 Sex Workers, 4 hours @$40/hr.	$4,800
Portfolio preparation	$3,000
Supplies (condoms, lubricant, etc.)	$3,000
Salaries for support staff: administration, Sex Worker training sessions, scheduling, logistics	$30,000

The services of the Sex Worker would be free to the client, but he would have to bear lodging and incidental costs for his venue of choice (e.g., a hotel suite). Of course the client could negotiate for further services, at his own expense, beyond the DESS sessions.

In general, American government agencies are confused and conflicted in their policies about human sexuality. Therefore, public funding of DESS programs could be problematical; better to seek initial funding from the private sector– foundations, philanthropists, gay community fundraisers, and suchlike. If DESS proves a success, the public sector may want to jump in, though perhaps at first with a judicious relabeling of workers as "consultants" to calm the anxieties of the more squeamish public officials.

Epidemiological Consequences

The goal is to achieve an enduring risk reduction of at least 50% in the high-risk clients, as a result of the IRRC + DESS intervention. Once word gets around the gay community, it's likely that DESS (a "tasty dessert") will serve as an incentive to undergo IRRC (a "nutritious dinner")– indeed, the enhanced recruitment to IRRC is a major benefit, quite apart from the learning benefit of DESS. It should not prove difficult to recruit 500 high-risk clients per year into the program; and in a few years, a majority of the City's high-risk men who have sex with men (MSM) will have had the intervention.

Making, then, three reasonable assumptions:

* The IRRC + DESS intervention permanently reduces risk by 50% among the collectivity of its clientele,
* At least half of San Francisco's high-risk MSM are included in the clientele within the first 3 years of operation,
* The high-risk MSM account for more than half of all risk posed by the sexual practices of MSM,

we can then estimate seroconversions avoided each year at a minimum of 1/2 x 1/2 x 1/2 of 748, or 93. Thus, an annual cost of $160,000 is matched against an eventual benefit of an annual minimum of 93 HIV infections avoided. That's a bargain, considering that about $10,000,000 is spent annually in San Francisco on HIV prevention.

Yet another benefit is to the morale of the Sex Worker staff: their DESS work would transform them from outcasts to heroes in the nation's fight against HIV disease. Perhaps, during Gay Pride Week of each year, they could be brought together for a testimonial dinner and civic awards. As they become more celebrated and legitimized, they might be convinced to lower their session fees to $150 or even $100. Of course, legitimization may mean Form 1099's for the Workers: a taxable portion of their professional income.

Stories from the Closet

My anecdotes are from a two-year period when I was completing undergraduate work and living in a fraternity on the north side of the UC Berkeley campus.

On my first day in the House, I met an 18-year-old freshman, George, who immediately intrigued me. Of course I was in the closet then, and for some years afterward, so nothing happened right off or for months afterward. In the Spring, though, the two of us were sitting on the stairway late at night after one of the fraternity's exuberant beer-keg parties. It was a warm evening; he looked great with his curly blond hair, lithe little body, and hairless legs exposed by shorts. I was so bold as to caress the back of his foreleg, gently, intensely. He gazed it me with equal gentle intensity; then we were interrupted and the moment of intimacy passed.

Six years later when I was a graduate student at Harvard, George came to visit. It was the winter after Stonewall, so it was now much easier to be frank. We had no trouble expressing our desire for one another, and spent a wonderful night together.

I lived in the fraternity house throughout the three semesters I attended UC. I joined for three main reasons: first, it was inexpensive room and board, close to the campus; second, it immediately provided a social environment that I liked; and third, it was the same fraternity that my Dad had belonged to when he was at Cal in the early 1920s.

The fact that the house was an all-male world was an added benefit, although homosexual attraction played a very much smaller role in my life than it did a few years later, i.e., in the three decades since Stonewall. My sexual desires were well sublimated into studies and other rewarding activities; this is evidenced by the fact that I had heterosexual intercourse only two or three times in those three semesters, and engaged in no homosexual activity at all (at least nothing more than my caress of young George's calf that Saturday night.) There were certainly some strong friendships in my life, as there were for most of the brothers– fraternity life was very much about forming such bonds, and many of them were profound and long-lasting. In my own strong friendships, sexuality played zero part.

My semesters at Cal was during the time just prior to the Free Speech Movement. There was a great deal of radical political activity on campus, which took different forms such as protest folksinging, or Beat nihilism, or civil rights activism. My fraternity brothers (as with the fraternity culture in general) had a mild disdain for all of this. We were very clear about sartorial distinctions: WE wore Madras shirts, short pants, and white socks, and had short haircuts; THEY wore colored socks and strange unhip shirts, and carried green book bags. But some of us were pretty leftist in our politics, and very sympathetic to civil rights for blacks, and certainly the majority of us would have voted for Jack Kennedy.

Bob, the cutest guy of all in our house, was also one of the most homophobic. He wasn't exactly hateful– his was far too sweet a temperament for that– but he expressed an almost instinctive disgust at any homoerotic expressions. Somehow we became good friends; there was a double-date to a prom that involved a long drive to Bakersfield and back, and there was another occasion in which we shared a double bed when we stayed over at another brother's house in San Francisco. Nothing ever happened between us– but there was one occasion, during Christmas break when only four or five of us were staying in the house, when Bob took it into his head to walk around the place totally nude. He (and the others of us) thought this was most amusing and daring.

Bill– tall, dark, strong, built like a Marine– was the most macho and masculine of all the brothers. He was the leader of many drunken capers, hilarious for their audacious vulgarity. Quite a number of these inebriated evenings would end with him putting a heavy make on one or another of the brothers. Chosen especially often for these unwanted attentions was my roommate Ted. Bill would pile on top of him in bed and make some very frank homoerotic advances, which Ted would resist with increasing vexation. Ironically, Ted was 100% heterosexual in spite of a theatrical voice, nicely-sculpted face, and reputation as one for whom "homosexuality/fits his personality" as was sung one afternoon (an adaptation of a song popular in our fraternity, itself an adaptation of a popular schoolkids' four-line song– the original (fraternity) opening lines were, "SAEs and Sigma Nus/Can hold a lot of booze".) Bill was never upbraided for his midnight homosexual playing because he was so obviously "straight".

There was another friend (not a Cal student), also in the closet, to whom I was not attracted but with whom I could at least talk about my gay feelings. He was more ashamed of his desires than I, and convinced me to see a psychologist for "therapy". The counseling was unmemorable– the counselor said little, as he was apparently of the "client centered" philosophy. I do recall that he was neither sympathetic nor judgmental. I quit after two sessions; even in 1963 I knew that I didn't really want to change.

Two of my fraternity brothers left the house to live together off-campus. Word soon got around that they were lovers;

this was a big scandal and it promptly divided the brotherhood into two halves, one unremittingly hostile and the other supportive to some degree. The attitudes of the latter were a mixture of respect for the courage of the pair of lovers, a general leftist-inspired feeling that people should be allowed to choose their own path, and simple liking for the two of them because (after all) they were a pair of decent handsome blond fellows. Much later I found out that one of the two had had sex with six of the brothers; perhaps this accounted for the (for those days) surprisingly extensive sympathy for an openly gay pair.

Of course there were gay jokes throughout my time in the house, but there was much less of a "what hateful deviants those guys are" quality than a "maybe you're that way too!" teasing-each-other quality. We were, after all, a group of 44 young men living together who often spoke of "loving our brothers." Machismo was fairly rare and restrained; ours was not one of the athletic, rough-housing fraternity cultures. The relative comfort we felt with our homosocial life was especially evident in February 1964, when Beatlemania arrived; one evening there were about 20 of us downstairs– we put on a just-acquired Beatles record– turned it up way loud– and danced with one another, laughing ecstatically.

Reflecting on all of this, I can see that it was fertile ground for the emergence of homosexual expression. Indeed, I was able to enjoy such emergence soon after, in London in the Summer of 1966 when I discovered the gay bars and after-hours clubs. What held me back at Berkeley– but not in London two years later– was the presence of so many fellows I knew and liked, whom I was sure would like me less if they found out I was gay.

V.

FUN AND GAMES

The notion of a 'simple, innocent childhood' is refuted in "The Innocent Pleasures of Adulthood". "Employee Burnout" and "Eulogical Workplace" delineate ten signs of, respectively, miserable and fabulous workplaces. "Zeno" takes 'After you, Alfonse'– 'No, no, after you, Gaston' to the final crunch. "Five-Handed Bridge" sets forth rules to enable five people to play America's favorite four-handed game. "Seven-Handed Bridge" does the same for a group of seven. "The Periodic Table" is a parochial view of the food elements which are the foundation of gustatory pleasure. "Intergalactic Purr" is about kitty's resonance with a universe-wide Intelligence. "Cat Lover/Cat Fanatic" enables demarcation between the two types of feline fancier. The "Syllabus" has prey and predator joining together for a day-long conference, including lunch, on the future of predation. "Why Can't a Dog Be More Like a Cat?" tells about that famous musical-comedy song from the 1940s.

TOOLS AND DEVICES
for the Executive to manipulate absent-mindedly
as he plays with the Salesman's business card
while listening to his Pitch

Pins
Scissors
Hole punch
"VOID" rubber stamp
Marker pens in various colors
Small Braun coffeebean grinder
Butter and butter knife
Cigarette lighter
Nitric acid bath

The Innocent Pleasures of Adulthood

One Spring afternoon, I was enjoying the Napa countryside in the company of my daughter Elizabeth, age six. The day was one of sublime beauty– an effulgence of greenery and wildflowers, soft breezes, birdsong near and far, puffy little white clouds– and I was content merely to sit on the porch of our farmhouse and drink it all in. I invited Elizabeth to do the same, but she would have none of it: her appetite was for games and toys and the collection of little bugs.

It occurred to me that, contrary to stereotypes, my enjoyment of the afternoon was genuinely simple and innocent. Elizabeth, on the other hand, was caught in a complex web of interests and feelings, with the constant threat of boredom or of tears-inducing frustration.

My great advantage, of course, was a lifetime of education and experience which provided me with a rich inner life that could resonate with the sublimity of the April environment. I needed very little, and there was no chance that I would be bored. Elizabeth was ill-furnished with an internal life and hence needed huge helpings of external entertainment. My son John, age nine months, seemed to be in an even more deprived, troubled state of mind: in his nearby cradle, he burst out with pathetic crying at regular intervals. Sad business for both children– but at least they can look forward to growing up to ever-increasing simplicity and innocence.

There's a nice distinction between *carefree* and *innocent* to be made here. Of course Elizabeth and John were care-free, whereas I had many cares: cook the meals, clean the house, do the driving, change the diapers, keep everyone healthy, and so forth. But once my chores were done, I could kick back. More to the point, I had the knack of meditation: I knew how to empty my mind of worries and obsessions, so that my minutes or hours of relaxation could be flooded with the healing, restoring, innocent, life-enhancing *bliss* of being-in-the-moment.

Ten Symptoms of Employee Burnout

(1) Tendency to vomit upon entering the workplace.

(2) In mind's eye, image of supervisor is inextricably blended with imagery of the Spanish Inquisition.

(3) On Sunday evenings, fall asleep crying;
on Monday mornings, wake up screaming.

(4) Fantasies about "calling in well" to work one morning, and never being seen again.

(5) Loss of bowel control during staff meetings.

(6) Uncontrollable laughter upon learning of the attempted suicide of a colleague.

(7) Total color-blindness while at work, followed by an immediate return of full color vision at 5 PM.

(8) A lunch-break reverie about winning the lottery, the reverie broken only by the realization that it's totally dark outside the cafe.

(9) Overweening joy when a client fails to show for an appointment.

(10) Excessive fascination with news reports of postal workers who shoot up their workplace. Obsession about route through the workplace, allocation of ordnance, hollow-point v. dum-dum, the when and where of reloading, possible spoken commentary, etc.

The Eulogical Workplace

The "frog in hot water" is a useful metaphor for our times: a frog dropped into a pan of hot water will hop out right away, but a frog placed in cool water that is very slowly heated will adapt to the imperceptible change in the environment and eventually boil to death. This metaphor can be applied to unhealthy work environments. An outside visitor would immediately notice the bad conditions, but an employee who has always been part of the environment simply adapts to the increasing and varied stresses, and barely notices that anything is wrong. Industrial psychologists have come up with various "markers" for unhealthy workplaces, using such measures as absenteeism, tardiness, frequent illnesses, breakdown in communication, etc. This analysis can be applied to dysfunctional families, whose members can long cleave to the conviction that their household is perfectly normal and happy.

But what about the opposite phenomenon, in which the work or family environment *enhances* health and harmonious functioning? This, too, could transpire without the participants' awareness, if they had "grown up with it." Just as industrial psychologists have developed markers for the pathological environment, there can be markers for the "eulogical" counterpart. These ten, I believe, are a good start:

(1) You tend to arrive to work early, relishing the challenges and vicissitudes of the day to come.

(2) Old friends say, "Hey, I didn't know that you...", and go on to speak of some talent, or interest, or accomplishment.

(3) Your winter colds, which used to hang on for four or five

days, now seem to go away after 24 hours.

(4) Some mornings, you wake up laughing.

(5) You have a distinct feeling of a romantic glow between yourself and several of your colleagues, even though no sexual attraction exists.

(6) The prospect of a pay raise, though welcome, simply isn't among your top priorities at work.

(7) *I slept, and dreamt that life was duty;*
I woke, and found that life was beauty.

(8) While commuting to work, you spend a lot of time musing about little ways you can bring joy to your colleagues– snacks, amusing newspaper clippings, a bouquet of flowers, humorous gifts, and so forth.

(9) When asked to describe your life or your world, you actually are tempted to express yourself in poetry or song– forms of expression which would amaze the people you went to school with.

(10) In reading about fictional or historical characters, you find that you consistently identify with the "winners".

As for the "eu-functional" family, one characterization comes to mind that sums it up nicely: "Gee, we never knew that we were poor– there was so much love, and we had such fun together!"

Zeno at the Intersection

When two drivers arrive simultaneously at an intersection, they often glance at one another for cues as to who should pass through first. Sometimes cues are misread and each proceeds simultaneously, upon which they look more closely for clearer cues. I propose a method whereby their standoff can be prolonged indefinitely, in the manner of "Zeno's Paradox". Zeno's Paradox is that a traveler can never get to his goal: once he is halfway there, he must go half the remaining distance; after which he must go half the remaining distance, and so on *ad infinitum*.

The "Zeno at the Intersection" method requires a beat-up old car and an "Actor" who *appears* to be in control of it. The car has one special feature, "Feedback Autopilot". Feedback Autopilot is initiated by targeting a nearby car with a laser beam. The direction and speed of the targeted car then determines, with nearly instantaneous response, the direction and speed of the vehicle controlled by the Autopilot.

Now picture an intersection with four-way stop signs. The Actor, heading north, arrives at the same moment as the Subject, heading east. At that moment the Actor locks the laser on to the Subject's car and initiates Autopilot. Feedback Autopilot thereafter runs the Actor's car as follows: any eastward movement of the Subject's car is exactly matched by northward movement of the Actor's car; likewise, each northward movement of the Subject's car is matched by eastward movement of the Actor's car. A minute's reflection will reveal that the movements of the Actor's car precisely mirror those of the Subject's car such that neither car can get beyond a diagonal line running between the southwest and northeast corners of the intersection. Thus, the Subject *cannot* continue east through the intersection: each time he moves forward a bit, the Actor's car does the same, its driver giggling with embarrassment at his apparent "stupidity".

The Actor's role will be to express himself good-naturedly, as cued by the mirrored movements of the two cars. He'll need a lot of "aw shucks, I'm such a klutz" facial expressions, in the style of Joe E. Brown or perhaps Jar-Jar Binks. But he'll admit no understanding of English; however much the Subject may gesticulate or shout, the Actor's only vocalizations will be in polite Bulgarian.

It is up to the Subject to terminate the interaction between the two vehicles. This can happen in four ways

(a) Subject's car turns north, Actor's car turns east.
(b) Subject's car U-turns and returns west, Actor's car U-turns and returns south.
(c) Subject's car stops and Subject emerges to confront the Actor.
(d) The two cars collide.

In cases (c) and (d), Subject and Actor will be able to meet in person. At that point, the Actor will reveal the true nature of the interaction and ask permission to conduct a brief physical examination– blood pressure, heart rate, urine sugar, serum testosterone level, etc.– that will help to determine whether "Zenotic" interactions of this sort increase or decrease stress. The Actor will then give a handsomely-printed tract on Zeno's Paradox to the Subject for his edification.

The Zeno at the Intersection paradigm is a marvelous design for examining how people handle frustration: when people are prevented from continuing in the desired direction, do they "press forward", "go around", or "stay put and wait"? Do they get upset, or adapt cheerfully? Do drivers in Manhattan, say, handle frustration differently from those in rural Minnesota?

Five-Handed Bridge

On occasion, five people will show up for an evening of bridge where only four were expected. Here is an adaptation of the game that enables all five to play at once.

Draw cards to determine partnerships. The two highest and two lowest each become partners, and the fifth becomes the "Booster". Seat the players around a pentagonal or a round table; the Booster may sit where he wishes, but partners should be separated by at least one other player.

Shuffle, cut, and deal the cards. Each player gets 10 cards; the two extra "Hole Cards" are put face down in the middle of the table. Dealer opens the bidding, which proceeds as in ordinary bridge except that the Booster remains silent. When the contract is agreed upon by three consecutive passes, the Booster then enters the bidding, but only to say either "pass" or "press on!" A "pass" ends the bidding, but a "press on!" reopens it. Bidding continues until *four* consecutive passes are heard.

When the final contract is set, the Booster distributes his hand to the other four players: three to the Declarer, three to the Dummy, and two to each Defender. The Booster does so with the aim of helping the contract to succeed. Then a Hole Card is given at random to each Defender. At this point, each player has 13 cards and play proceeds as in normal bridge.

The evening consists of 20 deals by the "Chicago" system, four by each of these combinations of the players A, B, C, D, and E:

Partnerships			Booster
A-B	v.	C-D	E
A-E	v.	B-C	D
A-D	v.	B-E	C
A-C	v.	D-E	B
B-D	v.	C-E	A

In each of the four deals of a set, neither team is vulnerable in the first hand, dealer's team is vulnerable in the second and third deals, and both teams are vulnerable in the fourth deal. There is no "above" or "below" the line, but a unitary score for one team: for the declarers if the contract is made, and for the defenders if it is set. For successful contracts, there is a 50-point bonus for part scores, 300 points for non-vulnerable games, and 500 points for vulnerable games. Slams and set contracts are scored as in normal bridge. Honors are not scored.

The Booster gets a positive score equal to that of the declaring team; but should the defenders prevail, he gets a *minus* score equal to their score. The Booster is motivated toward the success of a contract, and hence gives his best cards to the declaring team.

Each player's final score for the 20 deals, then, is a combination of his skills as Declarer, Defender, and Booster. A skillful Booster can do very well if he judges just how high to push a declaring team, in part because slams are not rare at Five-Handed Bridge.

Even though a hand as dealt has but 10 cards, and an average of 8 high card points, bidding can be aggressive: a declarer can expect the Booster's help both with high cards and distribution. Thus 10 points is ample to open the bidding, and a four-card suit is always biddable. A good strategy is to bid a hand as if it had 4 points more than it actually does. As for the Booster, a useful rule of thumb is to bid "press on!" once with 8 to 11 points, and twice with 12 or more points. In effect, the conventional Goren system is modified to create a useful bidding language for Five-Handed Bridge.

Of course, everyone should keep in mind that Hole Cards can bring *excellent* news to the Defenders...

Seven-Handed Bridge

Sometimes plans are made for an evening of two tables of bridge, but only seven people show up instead of the requisite eight. It's necessary to pick one person to be the "Sharpie", who will play at *both* tables. The Sharpie should be chosen, by secret ballot if necessary, for his/her competence and unflappability.

The Sharpie sits in the middle of the room on a swivel chair. Two bridge tables are placed on each side of the Sharpie, and three players are seated at each of these two tables. Play then proceeds as in normal bridge, with the Sharpie, in effect, simultaneously playing East at one table and West at the other.

The success of Seven-Handed Bridge depends upon the wit and alacrity of the Sharpie. This player has to manage two hands at a time, and occasionally has to be Declarer at both tables at once– all the while keeping up with the usual pleasant repartee of bridge ("Hey, don't rush me, I've only got two brains!")

The other players have the right to expect quick play from the Sharpie, so that the evening's games proceed as if there were actually eight people present. Much fun can be had with the "split personality" of the Sharpie, and with jests about him trying to switch cards ("Isn't that the second Ace of Trumps?") An ideal situation is where the Sharpie is a bisexual man, playing at one table with three women and at the other with three gay men.

Periodic Table of the Greatest Culinary Elements

MEATS	FISHES	MOLDS	LEAVES	BULBS	VEGE-TABLES	FRUITS	FLUIDS
1 **X** Chocolate "Meat of Life"							2 **Ch** Champagne "Fluid of Life"
3 **Fg** Foie Gras	4 **Cv** Caviar	5 **So** Sourdough	6 **Bl** Butter Lettuce	7 **Ga** Garlic	8 **S** Spinach	9 **Le** Lemon	10 **Yq** Sauternes
11 **La** Lamb	12 **Lo** Lobster	13 **Gg** Gorgon-zola	14 **Ag** Arugula	15 **P** Pepper	16 **Ap** Asparagus	17 **Rs** Raspberry	18 **Ca** Cabernet
19 **Du** Duck	20 **Sa** Salmon	21 **Pc** Porcini	22 **Ba** Basil		24 **Ar** Artichoke	25 **Tm** Tomato	26 **Pt** Port
27 **Fm** Filet Mignon	28 **Tu** Tuna	29 **Tr** Truffles	30 **Ci** Cilantro			33 **O** Olive	34 **Co** Cognac
						41 **Av** Avocado	42 **W** Whiskey

Tuning into the Intergalactic Purr

The carillonning of a cathedral's bells is a magnificent and inspiring experience. But a deaf man, sitting in his house at some distance from the cathedral, would notice nothing– unless he was able to *feel* it through resonance, for example by cupping a crystal goblet in his hands.

In just such a manner, we humans can become faintly aware of a certain Intelligence which suffuses our galaxy– specifically, the Intelligence peculiar to the feline civilizations that abound in the universe. In holding a purring cat in our hands, we acquire a vague, warm sense of that Intelligence: the purr is the dial-tone of a vast feline Internet.

Our deafness to this Intelligence is due to incomprehension of fundamental feline wisdom. For example, the essential purr-wisdom of *serene passion* escapes us; the very words seem oxymoronic. Of course, the catlike beings of the universe are equally uncomprehending of certain aspects of ape wisdom, especially in the matter of *self-deprecating humor,* which makes no sense at all to a feline mind. We have much to teach each other, if we would only tune in...

How to Distinguish a Cat Lover from a Cat Fanatic

Parameter	Cat Lover	Cat Fanatic
Essential attraction	The beauty and grace of cats	The *feline principle,* wherever expressed especially in such feline virtues as grace, arrogance, beauty, truculence, cleanliness...
Number of cats in household	One to four	Five or more– or zero ("Far too enamored of cats in general to make the mistake of loving one in particular")
Occasional pleasant fantasy...	...of actually having been a cat during a past life	...of actually having been a cat during this life
Age preference	Kittens to cats	Cats to kittens
Quote from landlord's ad	"...heat included. Cat OK. References required. For more information call...	"...heat included. Cat and references required. For more information call...

Attitude toward persistent meowing	Endures it for many minutes minutes before protesting	Prefers it to most, if not all, other background noises
Response upon learning ambassadors of an advanced feline civilization have landed on Earth and requested that all canines be locked up forthwith	"Why– this is amazing!"	"*There* you are– what took you so long?"

SYLLABUS

First North American Interspecies Conference on the Future of Predation

Tolman Hall, University of California, Berkeley
Monday, March 11, 1996

Time	Speaker	Topic
9:00-10:00	Dr. Seamus T. Squirrel	"Vegetarianism: Its Value in Physical and Psychological Health"
10:00-11:00	Professor P.M.W. Rabbit	"Toward a Harmonious and Nonviolent Forest Ecology"
11:00-12:00	Robin N. Sparrow, Esq.	"A New Methodology for Redirecting 'Innate' Aggression"
12:00-1:00	**L U N C H**	
1:00-2:00	Francis Fox, D.Litt.	"A Classical Essayist's Defense of the 'Good Old Ways'"

2:00-3:00	P. Barry Bobcat, Ph.D.	"Pitfalls in Adaptation to a Meatless Diet"
3:00-4:00	Professor Carol Eagle	"The Food Chain as an Expression of Psychosocial Balance"

Why Can't a Dog
Be More Like a Cat?

Notes on this songscript

"Why Can't a Dog / Be More Like a Cat?" is from Dogmalion, a musical comedy which enjoyed long runs in London (2,282 performances) and New York (2,718 performances) during the late 1940s. Dogmalion was one of the earliest collaborations of Alan Jay Lerner and Frederick Loewe.

The story of Dogmalion concerns an upper-class Englishman, George Gudger, who adopts an East End mongrel and attempts to train this dog to live with him in his Mayfair flat and to cope with the company of various pedigreed West End dogs. This training campaign has many ups and downs, whose humor is expressed musically in such still-famous songs as, "I Could Have Howled All Night", "With a Little Bit of Leash", "I'm Getting Neutered in the Morning", "Get Me to the Fireplug on Time", and "I've Grown Accustomed to Her Fleas". The piece I deal with here, "Why Can't a Dog / Be More Like a Cat?" occurs toward the end of the play: George, feeling that he has completed the education of his pet, has entered her in the Royal Belgravia Dog Show, where she has charmed everyone and swept highest honors. But the dog is distressed by George's aristocratic, unexpressive manner toward her, and, upon the chance appearance of her pack of East End mongrel old friends, has run off with them. This song is George's petulant expression to an acquaintance, Felix the cat.

"Why Can't a Dog / Be More Like a Cat?" depends for its comedic effect upon sprightly, staccato delivery on the part of the George Gudger character, and also upon the counterpoint provided by Loewe's brilliant instrumentation of clarinets, horns, trombones, and trumpets. The effect of the lyrics is to create a tense anticipation in the audience, something like, "My God– is this fellow going to turn out to be a cat lover?", which is later resolved.

The lead roles in the London production of Dogmalion were played by Ralph Richardson, Edith Evans, and Elassie Doglittle. The first performance took place at the Strand Theatre on October 31, 1947. Dogmalion enjoyed immense popularity on both sides of the Atlantic for many years, only recently being supplanted by Cats as the most celebrated "animal" musical in the English-speaking world.

During the 1950s, a clever parody of this song, titled "Why Can't a Woman/Be More Like a Man?" made the rounds. Of course, this parody's lyrics would today be considered sexist, if not downright vulgar. All printed copies were hunted down and burned by the National Organization for Women in the 1970s. However, I possess a handwritten copy that I will show to any visitor who attests that he or she is over 21 and of sound moral character.

John Newmeyer, Ph.D.
Music Historian

"Why Can't a Dog
Be More Like a Cat?"

[raucous barking offstage]

GUDGER: Felix, why can't a dog be more like a cat? Yes,

Why can't a dog
    be more like a cat?
Cats are so calm
    so tot'lly serene;
Eternally graceful
    historic'ly clean;
Whom did the Pharaohs revere?
    Why, the cat!
Why can't the dog
    be like that?

Why does ev'ry dog
    do what the others do?
Can't any mutt
    learn to shun the group?
Why can't just one pup
    try to do what you do?
Why don't they ever
    learn to bury their poop?

Why can't a puppy
    take after a cat?
Cats are so pleasant
    so easy to please.
Whenever you're with them
    they're always at ease.
Would you be slighted
    if I ignored you for weeks?

FELIX: Of course not!

GUDGER:

Would you be frantic
if I put you on the roof?

FELIX: Nonsense!

GUDGER:

Would you be wounded
if I never threw you sticks?

FELIX: Never!

GUDGER:

Why can't a dog
be aloof?!

One cat in a million
may yowl a bit.
Now and then there's one
with slight flaws yet;
One, perhaps, whose loyalty
you doubt a bit.
But by and large they
make a marvelous pet!

Why can't a canine
behave like a cat?
Cats are so placid
good natured and kind;

A better companion
you never will find.

If I were late for your walk
would you be whining?

FELIX: Of course not!

GUDGER:

If I forgot your silly
bath-day, would you hiss?

FELIX: Nonsense!

GUDGER:

Would you complain if I never
took you out driving?

FELIX: Never!

GUDGER:

Why can't a doggy,
be like this?!

Why can't a doggy
be more like a cat?
Cats are so elegant
such perfect artistes
Ready to help you
rise above the beasts.
Ready to bring out the prince
that's hidden inside.

Why can't a dog
have some pride?!

Why is grooming a thing
that dogs never do?
Why is licking
never even tried?
Chewing on their bones
is all they ever do.
Why don't they straighten
up the muss that's outside?

Why can't a doggy
be more like a cat?
If I were a mongrel
who'd been to a show,
Been hailed as a champion
by high and by low;
Would I start howling
like a coyote concert?
And carry on as if my
home were in a tree?

Would a pack of mangy old
mutts tempt me to revert?
Why can't a doggy
be like me?!

Pets and Spiritual Health

There are many ways that pets contribute to our physical and mental health. They amuse us and give us exercise. They provide companionship, especially important in an era when so many households consist of just one person. And merely petting a cat or dog can lower one's blood pressure. The relevance of pets to health is such that it is now standard practice for eldercare homes to provide dogs and cats to keep people healthy and connected with life.

But I'd like to go a step further and suggest that living with a dog or cat is good for *spiritual* health. In different ways, dogs and cats can augment our religious experience.

The dog is the supreme teacher of the kindergarten lesson, "God is love", fundamental to Christian worship. For thousands of years, abundant love has been integral to human/canine bonding. Of course, the dog is subordinate in the loving relationship, but his unconditional loyalty and devotion is akin to the Islamic and Christian notions of submission to God. As our canine friend puts his loving trust in us, so we put our loving trust in a higher power.

By contrast, companionship with a cat opens one to the more meditative, reflective, inward-looking forms of religious experience– and a more abstract, depersonalized sense of the higher power. To watch a cat compose herself is to be put in mind of the Taoist or Buddhist becoming quiet and centered, emptying the mind of distractions, and allowing the ineffable life force to flow unimpeded. In the solitary feline calm is the same calm oneness with God of silent prayer. And in the cat's purr we have the Om of the Hindu: cat and devotee are each resonating with the "dial-tone of the universe."

The simple act of committing ourselves to care for a pet– or a child– is really the heart of the matter. Our tender regard for another creature's life and wellbeing, and our loving affirmation of that life, may be all we need to know of God.